# Parenting in
# Transracial Adoption

*Real Questions and*
*Real Answers*

JANE HOYT-OLIVER,
HOPE HASLAM STRAUGHAN, AND
JAYNE E. SCHOOLER

 PRAEGER™

An Imprint of ABC-CLIO, LLC

Santa Barbara, California • Denver, Colorado

**Library of Congress Cataloging-in-Publication Data**

Names: Hoyt-Oliver, Jane, author. | Straughan, Hope Haslam, author. | Schooler, Jayne E., author.
Title: Parenting in transracial adoption : real questions and real answers / Jane Hoyt-Oliver Ph.D., Hope Haslam Straughan Ph.D., Jayne E. Schooler.
Description: Santa Barbara : Praeger, 2016.
Identifiers: LCCN 2015037395 | ISBN 9781440837029 (hardback) | ISBN 9781440837036 (ebook)
Subjects: LCSH: Interracial adoption. | Parenting. | BISAC: FAMILY & RELATIONSHIPS / Adoption & Fostering. | PSYCHOLOGY / Developmental / Adolescent. | PSYCHOLOGY / Developmental / Child.
Classification: LCC HV875.6 .H69 2016 | DDC 649/.145— dc23 LC record available at http://lccn.loc.gov/2015037395

ISBN: 978-1-4408-3702-9
EISBN: 978-1-4408-3703-6

20  19  18  17  16    1  2  3  4  5

This book is also available on the World Wide Web as an eBook.
Visit www.abc-clio.com for details.

Praeger
An Imprint of ABC-CLIO, LLC

ABC-CLIO, LLC
130 Cremona Drive, P.O. Box 1911
Santa Barbara, California 93116-1911

This book is printed on acid-free paper ∞
Manufactured in the United States of America

To my husband and our wonderful daughter: we journey together in love and I am grateful for the walk every day. To our parents Barbara and Newton Hoyt and Helen and Leon Oliver: your love provided our family both roots and wings. To my brother Robert and sister Ann, without whom growing up would have been far lonelier and much less exciting. And finally to those who create forever families through adoption.

—Jane Hoyt-Oliver

To my husband and beautiful sons, thank you for being my forever family, and all that it means. To our extended family, family through our adopted sons, dear friends, and social service support partners who journey along with us, I give my sincere thanks and gratitude for all that you bring to our lives and to my exploration of the ideas contained in this book. To my co-authors, I offer extraordinary gratitude for the privileged, beautiful, and intense journey we have undertaken, and the supports you have been to me throughout.

—Hope Haslam Straughan

To Betsy Keefer Smalley, thank you for your ever constant support, enthusiasm, and commitment to the vision of writing to help adoptive families for many years. You have touched lives around the world. Thank you for never saying no when an idea is passed your way!

—Jayne E. Schooler

# Contents

# Acknowledgments

I would like to thank the staff at ABC-CLIO, especially our editor Debbie Carvalko, for their help and support throughout this process. This book would not have been possible without Ms. Carvalko's enthusiasm for our project. The generous support of Malone University was critical; a faculty research grant as well as a semester-long sabbatical provided me with the time to write. Becky Albertson transcribed our interviews with precision; thank you, Becky, for your steadfast work. In addition, the encouragement and backing of faculty in both the departments of Social Work and History/Philosophy/Social Sciences at Malone University often provided inspiration. I admire and thank you all.

—Jane Hoyt-Oliver

I have learned so much from hearing the narratives of the many parents who graciously took part in our study, as I've continued to navigate my own transracially adoptive parenting journey. I want to thank those families, and especially recognize the strengths noted when asked how they'd changed due to being a transracially adoptive parent. The generous support of Wheelock College was critical, specifically providing research grants to pay for transcription. I would also like to thank Debbie Carvalko at ABC-CLIO for her guidance and support.

—Hope Haslam Straughan

Without the families who so freely and openly shared their stories, we would not have the wealth of insight we have gained. I would like to thank those families who shared what life experiences have taught them. I also would like to thank Debbie Carvalko and the team at ABC-CLIO for their high level of professionalism and guidance.

—Jayne E. Schooler

# Introduction

## JANE HOYT-OLIVER

———————————————————————————————— ᔕ

*Do parents discuss what they believe about race and culture before they adopt?*

*Do they talk about race and culture within their extended family before they adopt?*

*Do issues of race and cultural emerge for adoptive parents for which they feel unprepared?*

It is these questions and many more which are the subject of this book. In recent decades, researchers have been interested in the effects of transracial adoption on the adoptees. Some of the most poignant writings have been authored by the adoptees themselves (Hofmann, 2010). A good deal of past research emphasis has been placed on the experiences of children who have been adopted from other countries (Simon & Roorda, 2000). A few studies have focused on in-country transracial adoption (Alexander & Curtis, 1996).

From a recognition of the reality of cultural disruption (Simon & Alstein, 1996), to the newly emerging study of the role that trauma plays within the adoption process, social workers and parents have begun to address the expressed needs of adoptees (Schooler, Smalley, & Callahan, 2010). But little research has been conducted to understand how adopting parents view themselves, or how their worldview may affect the family dynamics.

As with many decisions, the reasons that families adopt can be as varied as the families themselves. Some potential parents may want to expand their family by adoption because they cannot biologically have children. Others may feel they have been successful parents to biological children and believe they have "more to give" as parents. Still others make the choice to adopt for religious reasons, believing that adoption is a way to demonstrate the love of God for all people and an alternative to abortion (Brown, 2012). That's where parents begin. But, as with many adult "whole life" decisions (others can include who to marry or, increasingly, *whether* to marry, how to express one's sexuality, how one balances work requirements and home life, or whether to divorce), people often enter lifelong decisions with limited information. "I wish I had known . . ." sometimes seems to be the universal cry of parenthood.

Of course, there are things we simply can't know until we have lived them. For example, there are many books on the market that discuss steps one might take to have a long and happy marriage, and many of those books provide great advice. But long-term partners will acknowledge that all the books in the world could not have prepared them completely to BE lifelong partners. A book's suggestions can help, but true grounded learning occurs when knowledge is combined with experience. It takes working it out in action on the part of both partners to accomplish the goal of a strong and steady relationship.

We believe this is true of adoption and child rearing as well. The work of raising children is the work of parents as they are living in a community. But information also helps. This book is designed to help parents who wish to adopt transracially (as well as the caring professionals who assist them with the process) to consider some of the very real issues that arise when children are raised in multiracial households.

Adoption, by definition, brings people together who choose to merge their histories and life understandings. This is never an easy task. In the previous century, adoption experts believed that the trauma associated with adoption could be minimized if the children were adopted as infants. Recent research regarding the traumatic impact of adoption even in infancy point to this being a simplistic belief at best and deeply misguided at its worst (Johnson, 2002; Solchany, 2014).

In addition to issues that arise during every adoption, research has shown that parents who adopt transracially have additional issues to address (Quiroz, 2007). These adopting parents, their children, and the extended biological families are confronted with how to understand race within the context of the family and within the context of their communities.

Adopting parents want to be good parents. It is our belief that honest discussion of the issues raised by this book can assist parents to meet that goal.

All of the authors have transracial children or grandchildren within their immediate or extended families. Having met through professional contacts, they found themselves carving out time to talk about parenting, adoption, and issues of race.

As they researched the topic of transracial adoption, they discovered that there was a good deal of information from a *child's* perspective regarding transracial adoption, but there was little research published regarding *parental perspectives* about race and culture. The authors understood through their professional practice experience that parents' current reactions to the stressful circumstances of parenting are not simply based on the events themselves but also what they bring from their own life experiences.

Experiences growing up shape one's view of oneself, others, and the community. For example, when one of the authors was in elementary school, she had a lesson at home and in school about the safety of authority figures. She recalls being told by teachers and her parents that if there was trouble, she should "find a policeman." The implicit (and often explicit!) message was that the policeman would not only listen to her concern, but would take it seriously. Indeed, it was assumed that the police would protect her from danger if her parents could not. The larger cultural assumption was authorities are to be trusted and were also trustworthy. Many Caucasian parents trust in that message and they pass it down to their children. But can this seemingly basic message be generalized across racial lines?

For example, in 2012, Treyvon Martin, a young unarmed African American teen, was killed walking to his mother's home after buying snacks at a local convenience store. During the investigation and the trial that followed, many in the media reported wide disparities between how Caucasian Americans viewed the situation as compared to African Americans. When the shooter was acquitted, *Washington Post* writers Jon Cohen and Dan Balz reported "87% [of African Americans] believed the shooting was unjustified. In contrast, 51% of whites approved of the verdict while just 31% of whites disapprove[d]" (2013).

Reflecting on the verdict, an African American friend of one of the authors noted, "Trevyon could have been my son. He could be any African American parent's son." For this man, Martin's death was reminiscent of white America's legacy of arbitrary violence and oppression of Americans of African descent.

Many African American parents took time to discuss this situation with their children: to talk about strategies for dealing with the sometimes capricious and often random scrutiny that children of color face in many areas of the country.

The deep contrasts between the reactions of African American and Caucasian parents is important to the central theme of this book, because white parents who adopt transracially must be willing to understand both the realities of the prominently white-oriented culture in which they have grown up and how their children of color are seen in that world. These adopting parents, their children, and the extended biological families are confronted with how to understand race within the context of the family and within the context of their communities. It is especially important for transracially adopting parents to critically consider how they have conceptualized race, how they plan to address the issue of race within their families, and how they will prepare their children for a world that continues to stratify people along racial lines.

The foundation of this book is a multiple year study which the authors undertook to understand how parents who have adopted transracially think about race and culture. The authors conducted in-depth interviews with 13 couples in Ohio and Massachusetts. Each member of the couple was interviewed separately so that both parents could share their own understanding of the experience of parenting. Eleven of the couples were heterosexual and married; two were in long-term same-sex partnerships.

Questions utilized during the interviews included:

In what ways did you think about culture and race before you were an adoptive parent?
Describe the process of your decision to become a transracially adoptive parent.
How have issues of culture and race come up for you as an adoptive parent?
In what ways has being a transracially adoptive parent changed you?
Is there anything else you would like to add regarding race and culture in regards to your experience as a transracially adopting parent?

The interviews lasted for between 45 minutes and 2.5 hours. Parents spoke candidly about where and how they grew up, the influences upon their lives, and the decision to adopt transracially. Each told their story of both the joys and the painful realities of parenting trans-racially. We were honored that they trusted us with their stories.

After completing the interviews and having them transcribed into written form, we met as a team to listen and to learn from the parents about how they understood race and culture as children. We looked for themes that might transcend individual interviews and for the wisdom that comes from experiencing the world in a way that many of the parents had not considered when growing up in a predominantly white world. To these themes, we have added some of the latest research to assist parents and practitioners to make wise decisions. These themes make up the chapter titles of this book. The themes include:

## IN HER VOICE: MICHELLE

From experiences as early as elementary school, Michelle shares her insights on what it was to grow up as a transracially adopted person in predominately white communities. She relates events that happened, her perceptions of those events, and how they have shaped her in becoming the young woman she is today.

## I NEVER THOUGHT ABOUT RACE GROWING UP

All of the parents in our study grew up in predominantly white communities. When asked about how they understood race when they were young, few of the parents interviewed in our study "thought about race" when they were growing up. Only one of the parents interviewed could recount a situation which was identified as a "racist incident" in the neighborhood, but many parents recounted growing up in families whose adult members were vocally racist. This chapter will explore how parents' early years appear to impact their understanding of parenting and some of the unique challenges parents faced when adopting.

## DEALING WITH RACE IN THE EXTENDED FAMILY AND COMMUNITY

Adopting transracially doesn't just touch the lives of the adoptive parents and child, but has a much wider impact on others as well.

This chapter examines the need for adoptive parents to think about the issues of races within the context of the extended family and within the context of the wider community in which the child and family live. Offering strategies for having those needed conversations within family is discussed as well as offering ways to help parents think about the concept of race within their own community

## HAIR AS A METAPHOR: ENTERING INTO THE CULTURE OF YOUR CHILD

Parents who adopt transracially face a number of issues that may not arise if one adopts a child of the same race. One area that is often mentioned is the issue surrounding grooming: white parents may not know how to care well for the hair of their children. Options might include: "pretending" that there is no difference in the grooming needs of the child; asking assistance from the members of the African American community to learn to care for the child's hair (which sometimes may reinforce to the parent that s/he is not the birth parent and can increase anxiety about overall parenting skills); or finding a barbershop/hairdresser who can do a professional job (which for some parents means that they experience going to a rarely visited part of their community in which they do not "feel welcome"). We believe such issues surrounding grooming are both a concrete reality and a metaphor for some of the difficult emotional terrain that transracially adopting parents must navigate—not only within themselves and with their children but within the wider communities in which they live. Discussing these issues can provide strategies by which parents can become a part of their child's world, not simply expect the child to enter the parent's world

## IN HIS VOICE: KEVIN

Kevin's experiences growing up as a transracially adopted person in both predominately white and predominately African American communities has given him unique insight and understanding. He shares those events that happened, his perceptions of those events, and how they have shaped him in becoming the insightful man he is today.

## PARENTING BETWEEN CULTURES: IMPORTANT CONSIDERATIONS FOR PARENTS

This chapter focuses on three important aspects of parenting: the development of a child's identity, formation of self-esteem, and issues of power.

## PARENTING A TRANSRACIALLY ADOPTED CHILD WITH A HISTORY OF TRAUMA

Many children who are adopted transracially through the foster care system not only face challenges of adoption and growing up in a transracial adoptive family, but challenges related to overcoming the impact of trauma, neglect, and loss. This chapter explores this critical area parents need to understand in addition to understanding issues of cultural and race.

## ADOPTION COMMUNICATION WITHIN THE TRANSRACIAL ADOPTIVE FAMILY

Talking about adoption issues, birth parents, a child's history, and possible traumatic events is a requirement for any adoptive family. However, there is an additional layer of communication that is needed for adoptive families of transracially adopted children. This chapter explores that extra layer of communication and provides practical advice and questions for discussion by those who might be considering transracial adoption and for those already living in the context of a transracial family.

## IN HER VOICE: ANGELA

Much like Michelle and Kevin in earlier chapters, Angela's story shares her experiences growing up with Caucasian parents. An added experience Angela shares is the story of reunion with both her African American biological parents.

## CONVERSATIONS WITH PRACTITIONERS: WHAT ADOPTION PROFESSIONALS WANT PARENTS TO CONSIDER

Research for this book brought us in contact with many professionals interested in adoption. We interviewed a number of adoption caseworkers to find out what they wished that parents adopting transracially would consider both BEFORE they adopt and AFTER the adoption is final. This chapter summarizes their insights and can provide opportunities for some important conversations between adopting parents and between parents and the social workers who will be assisting them to adopt.

This work has been an exciting adventure for all of us. We hope that this book will help practitioners to ask the best questions as they consider who might be best suited to adopt a child on their caseload. In addition, we hope that the material will assist potential adopting parents to think about the issues of race carefully as they consider adoption. We pray that it will inspire you to many deep and honest conversations with each other, with relatives, neighbors, friends, and with spiritual leaders. Adopting a child is both intensely personal and a community decision. Preparing well is one way to face the challenges ahead.

## BIBLIOGRAPHY

Alexander Jr., R., & Curtis, C. M. (1996). A review of the empirical research involving the transracial adoption of African American children. *Black Psychology, 22*(2), 223–235.

Brown, C. B. (2012). Why do more people choose abortion over adoption? *Lifenews.com*. Retrieved from http://www.lifenews.com/2012/05/17 /why-do-more-people-choose-abortion-over-adoption/

Cohen, J. & Balz, D. (2013). Zimmerman verdict poll: Stark reaction by race. *Washington Post*. Retrieved from http://www.washingtonpost .com/politics/race-shapes-zimmerman-verdict-reaction/2013/07/22 /3569662c-f2fc-11e2-8505-bf6f231e77b4_story

Hofmann, K. D. (2010). *Growing up black in white*. Toledo, OH: The Vine Appointment Publishing Company.

Johnson, D. E. (2002). Adoption and the effect on children's development. *Early Human Development, 68*(1), 39-54.

Quiroz, P. A. (2007). *Adoption in a color-blind society*. Lanham, MD: Rowman & Littlefield Publishers.

Schooler, J. E., Smalley B. K., & Callahan, T. J. (2010). *Wounded children, healing homes: How traumatized children impact adoptive and foster families*. Colorado Springs, CO: Nav Press, Inc.

Simon, R. J., & Altstein, H. (1996). The case for transracial adoption. *Children and Youth Services Review, 18*(1/2), 5–22.

Simon, R. J., & Roorda, R. M. (2000). *In their own voices: Transracial adoptees tell their stories*. New York: Columbia University Press.

Solchany, J. (2014). Forming a healthy attachment with your adopted child. *Baby Center*. Retrieved from www.babycenter.com/0_forming -a-healthy-attachment-with-your-adopted-child_137

# CHAPTER 1

# In Her Voice: Michelle

MICHELLE OLIVER

*What is the best way adoptive parents can learn about the needs of their transracially adoptive children? The answer is simple. Listen to them. Michelle's story is the first of three stories about growing up as a transracial adopted person.*

## CREATING AN IDENTITY

"Why are you black?" A boy in my third grade class asked me this question innocently enough. But the *way* he said it made it feel like being "black" was something bad, like having cooties or smelling funny. This was the first encounter I can recall with any real concept of race. Before that time, I was just one of the rest of the kids living in a rural, small, predominately white town in Ohio. I was one of two or three minority students in the entire school, the rest being Caucasian. After my classmate's comment, I decided I did NOT want to be black, whatever that meant.

I had not really given any thought before to the color of my skin, or that of my adoptive parents. My birth mother surrendered me for adoption when I was born, and my new parents, a Caucasian couple living in rural Ohio, made me part of their family when I was three months old. My adoptive father was a minister, and my adoptive mother was employed with a local hospice. They loved me and I loved them. We were a family. We had friends who were Caucasian from our rural community, friends from New England where both my parents were from, and also friends who were of different religions, different skin tones, and came from different parts of the world. But up until a certain point in time, I hadn't really thought too much about those differences as being significant or having positive or negative connotations. But then came that day in school that I will never forget. That question: *Why are you black?*

I learned later in third grade history class about world civilizations, and began to recognize that there were different shades and cultures of people out there in the world, and started to look at my skin in comparison to my classmates. Then, I met the only other brown girl in my school, who declared to me that she was Salvadoran—and proud of it! I knew she was different, and I was brown too, so I was probably different, but I didn't have some proud country of heritage to claim, to explain my brown skin.

So, in the third grade, I subconsciously came up with my very own explanation for my brownness. As we had learned about the Egyptian civilization in history class, I gathered that the Egyptians were a powerful, important, and wealthy group of folks. This was reinforced by our visits to history museums when we visited my parents' families on the East Coast. So somewhere in that time frame I created an identity for myself—I was part Egyptian. I really believed this. My brain registered me as being Egyptian, and in my mind I was convinced that my adoptive parents[1] had even told me I was of Egyptian heritage, even though this never happened in real life. My parents had told me that I was part white, part black, and part Asian when I was younger. But my own creation of identity somehow trumped any such explanation, right there in the third grade.

If anyone would ask what ethnicity or race I was, I would tell them Egyptian. This self-created identity was so strong, that it was not until my sophomore year of high school that I actually realized I *wasn't* Egyptian. By that time, I had actually gained more confidence in the way I looked, in being different and "exotic looking" and in being multiracial, so it was not a big deal to rediscover my authentic ethnic makeup. Although it's more of a funny story for me now, I still marvel at the fact that I had created this identity for myself. This likely stemmed from a desire to: (a) not be "black," because the kid on the playground seemed to think being black was "bad," and (b) have a proud heritage of a proud people that I could enthusiastically exclaim to any inquiring minds, just like my friend of Salvadoran descent did to me.

Egypt is a country in Africa, and we all know that most "black" people (as we refer to ourselves in America) came from Africa. But as I learned later in college, Northern African folks don't really consider themselves black. This is more a term utilized for sub-Saharan Africans, and, of course, African Americans. That tidbit I didn't consciously learn until college. But somehow I knew this in the third grade, and felt it was OK to be Egyptian, but not OK to be "black."

## MY THOUGHTS FOR PARENTS

*My advice to white parents adopting interracially would be to, very early on, explain how there are different races and ethnicities of people, and they are all equally great and wonderful. Talk with your child a bit about their ethnic makeup or heritage. If this is not immediately or precisely known, that's OK, you can start to decipher what race your child identifies him or herself as. Or, after explaining some of the different races and ethnicities of people in America and around the world, ask your child if he or she has any questions. If a child asks why her skin looks different, or what it means to be "black," as a parent be prepared to have this conversation.*

It was very beneficial that my parents had a number of genuine friends of different races—African, African American, Central European, and Asian. My mom's cousin had married a man from Japan, so when I was with their daughter, we could connect. Being able to talk with these friends of my parents and—even better—their children did so many positive things for me. For example, friends from Africa who were so confident and enthusiastic about their Nigerian heritage gave me a sense of pride in who they were. In addition to our Nigerian friends, I remember being in awe of some friends of my grandmother. They were originally from India and were very prominent in my grandmother's community. They lived in a beautiful home with impressive Indian décor—getting to know these two families from vastly different cultures, but who were both "brown" like me had a lasting impression on me because I was able to associate brown folks with pride, prominence, and sophistication.

## EXPERIENCING RACISM AND PREJUDICE

If adoptive parents bring a child of color into the family, they can be quite sure that their child will experience some form of racism and/or prejudice. This may be overt or subtle. This is not something parents need to be afraid of; it is something you will want to prepare for. The more parents are aware of some of the possible experiences a child will face, the more they can be proactive in offering love and support when painful situations arise. Make sure there is time around the dinner table to talk about the joys and pains of the day or if the news discusses an issue of race, bring it up for discussion during family time. And parents need to be alert: because sometimes painful things happen that your child may not want to discuss. These experiences come from many different places and people.

## HEARING THE N-WORD ON THE PLAYGROUND

I was called the N-word on the playground in sixth grade. We were playing a game of kickball on the playground, and a Caucasian boy in my class who was known as sort of rough around the edges and as somewhat of a bully, was angry about a play called in my favor and came up to me and along with a string of expletives called me something to the effect of "stupid nigger." I'm not exactly sure how I knew what that word meant (possibly because I had already been exposed to some documentaries and writings on the Civil Rights Movement by mom and dad), but I did and it cut like a knife.

Those around us on the playground fell silent and stared at me, wondering what I would do. They did not defend me or yell at the boy. I was so angry and hurt that I punched him, and the recess monitor had to separate us. I don't remember if the boy was punished but I know I was; I had to stand in time out for the rest of recess and get a stern talking to by the teacher. I was so ashamed of what the boy had called me that I kept it to myself and didn't say why I had punched him. That carried over after I went home that day—I didn't tell my parents, and the school didn't tell them I had gotten in trouble. The shame of being called that word as a child, in a small town community that was 99% white was the worst part of the experience. The shame that I was associated with that word was terrifying, so I didn't tell anyone.

## NAVIGATING THROUGH THE SHAME

The good news is that the boy (from the first N-word incident on the playground) and I did not remain hostile for long. I remember there was a general opportunity at my church offered to us in a message to forgive those who have hurt us. I felt in my heart I needed to forgive him. Even as a youth, I was beginning to understand that hurt people hurt people, and my eyes were opened to the fact that this boy was not inherently a horrible person, but he was reacting to being upset at me in a manner that was familiar to him. In addition, this young man came from a very broken home. I was able to forgive him in my heart. Eventually the whole thing passed without much more being said. And the important part was that I was not harboring bitterness in my own heart.

I learned, primarily through talks with my parents about faith and about forgiveness as well as through mentors and Sunday school teachers at church who took an interest in my character development, that the most lasting "remedy" for that pain on the inside, for me, would *not* have been vengeance—that is, watching the boy get severely punished and shamed for what he did to me. That would have felt good for a moment, but then the situation would have soured and it would not have resolved the "yuck" I felt on the inside. In fact, that might have created a deeper chasm between myself and the boy and other white boys in the future. I would have harbored bitterness against them that could have carried over into adulthood.

Several years later, I was mowing the lawn when I felt something wet on my face. Another young troublemaker had driven by in a car- and I was sure he had spit on me. I started to cry and my dad, who was close by, asked what had happened. When he heard, he was furious and we went to the police station and Dad filed a report (it was a *very* small town and my dad was one of three pastors in the community). The police took Dad's complaint seriously and within an hour, the young man and his father were at our house and he offered an apology. I learned then that my parents would protect me when they could.

I recognize that not every racially-charged situation like the ones above will have such a positive or seemingly "easy" ending (though I will tell you that these experiences were not easy for me). People say and do extremely hurtful things, lashing out at those of other races. Blacks in this country have gone through lynching, segregation, police brutality, and much more. Yet many powerful leaders in the black community agree that it can be debilitating and unfruitful to harbor bitterness and resentment on the inside, even when it appears to be justified against an oppressor.

I find inspiration, and a way of holding such experiences in a healthier, more compassionate way, through the work of people like Nelson Mandela, Maya Angelou, and Dr. Martin Luther King, Jr. Nelson Mandela, when asked why he was not resentful for his imprisonment, said, "resentment is like a glass of poison that a man drinks; then he sits down and waits for his enemy to die." Maya Angelou wrote, "We cannot change the past, but we can change our attitude toward it. Uproot guilt and plant forgiveness. Tear out arrogance and seed humility. Exchange love for hate—thereby, making the present comfortable and the future promising." Dr. Martin Luther King said, "forgiveness is not an occasional act; it is a permanent attitude." I agree with these sentiments and have tried to live my life by these principles. But growing up, there was sometimes a fine line between feeling confident about who I am and feeling like I was different.

## FEELING SINGLED OUT

My eighth grade history teacher was a woman whom I greatly admired. She was trying her very best to teach a unit on slavery in America, despite the fact that our textbooks only gave about a sentence of space to the topic. I believe what she was trying to do was very important and necessary—all children need to learn about and discuss this important aspect of history in our country. However, I remember we were in the middle of a lesson about slavery and the hardships African Americans faced, when she turned to me and asked, "Michelle, what do *you* think about this? How does this make you feel?"

My teacher might have been calling on me randomly, but since I was the only child to get called on and I was the only person of color in the room, I felt singled out. I felt a lump in my throat, and didn't really know what to say. Was she calling on me so I could relay to the others how it feels to be black and to listen to the reality of oppression and subjugation? How was I as a 13-year-old child supposed to respond to such a question with no preparation? Did she expect me to speak for myself or for all people of color? It was a strange experience and I was uncomfortable. But even beyond that moment, as a person who considers herself African American, I know that almost every time up until the end of high school whenever Jim Crow, or slavery, or racism in America was discussed in school, I couldn't help but feel that all eyes were staring at me.

It's important to note that my uncomfortable feeling is not the major takeaway from this vignette. The greater thing to highlight was the deep connection I felt in my soul with the suffering and challenges blacks in this country have gone through when I started learning about it in history classes, and also from the educational resources my parents had me read and watch, as well as the discussions they had with me about these things. There is pain that many black kids will feel when learning about these things that happened in America—more so than white children.

## MY THOUGHTS FOR PARENTS

*If your child considers themselves African American, they will most likely connect with the struggles blacks had in America, and the connection with these struggles may cause internal hurt, anger, and a feeling of disconnection or disenfranchisement with "white" America. It is important to talk about what your child is experiencing as they learn these aspects of history and processes through it. Grieve with them, acknowledge that the things that have happened in this country are wrong, and have repercussions today, and we all have a role in making today's society better. Learn to recognize that there are vast and painful gaps in history that exclude people of color and gloss over their achievements.*

## EXPERIENCING SUBTLE RACISM

Some experiences I would coin "subtle racism" occurred as well. As a parent of a minority person, you will need to be ready to discuss these types of scenarios with your child. Listen carefully and be aware that these racially charged situations arise even in the seemingly "safest" community. Be alert if your child is beginning to withdraw from deeper conversations or withdraw generally into themselves—the child may have experienced a situation where they were made fun of or singled out. Be ready to talk about the realities of unkindness—kids, adolescents, and adults alike can all say unkind things and point out differences in others, and these unkind actions may be based on the target person's race or gender.

There were a couple of occasions when I would be out at an upscale restaurant with my parents and my dad's extended family—all white—and the host would ask my parents if I was with them, thinking I, then about 20, was the nanny. This also happened while summering in an upscale part of New England—I was mistaken for the family nanny. It stung me and is also indicative of the fact that interracial families are still more uncommon than not. The antidote here was my family somewhat disdainfully remarking to the server that, yes, of course, she's our daughter. That made me feel better.

I can remember experiences that were probably *not* someone being racist, but instead me dealing with insecurities. There was an experience I had being part of the school cheerleading squad. For one of the seasons I cheered, I was the only non-white cheerleader on the team and perhaps even the only non-white, non-blond cheerleader. I was never, ever, put in the front row of our cheerleading formation—I was always in the back. Same with squad photos—always in the back. I was never featured in the special parts of our routines. Now, I was also probably one of the taller ones so perhaps it made sense for me to be in the back, and admittedly, I was not the most talented tumbler or jumper on the squad, so there are likely pragmatic reasons that I was placed where I was. But I didn't feel I could ask why I was not featured and at that age clearly was reluctant to have my parents ask for me. So it became a lingering internal hurt.

This experience was coupled with the fact that it was always the pretty, blond-haired, blue-eyed girls on the squad who were getting all the attention from the boys. I found myself being annoyed with boys— why wouldn't they notice me? Perhaps they were racist jerks, right? But along with the defiant thoughts were the insecure ones, the thoughts that whispered I was not blond enough, that I was not pretty, and that my curly hair would be nicer if it was straight. I got colored contacts, dyed my hair with bright blond highlights, and would look through the teen fashion magazines longingly, wishing I looked like some of the blond models all over the pages.

It wasn't until later in high school, after my family moved to a more diverse setting, that I started to have friends of different races who had confidence and thought women of color were the most beautiful creatures on earth. I remember thinking that in my new community, there was a different standard of beauty and I came closer to that new standard! I blossomed in this more diverse environment. This confidence was infectious, and it was those girl friends who emanated confidence in being black and brown, and who influenced me and helped me love the way I look. The boys started noticing me too (probably more as a result of my new found confidence), but as I explain to younger girls that I now mentor—building one's confidence on the compliments and advances of boys is a very, very bad idea.

These issues don't just occur when children are young. There were a few occasions when peers in high school and even law school questioned whether I received certain opportunities on my own merits.

One girl in law school—a childhood friend nonetheless—commented that I probably was chosen for a particularly competitive summer clerkship so that the firm could fulfill a diversity objective. An offer was not extended to her. She believed we were at about the same level academically, so, of course, the only reason in her mind that she wasn't chosen was that I was a minority.

It did not appear that she understood how hurtful her comment was! I remember telling my mom about the experience, and she reminded me that though this girl looked Caucasian, she also came from a diverse ethnic background. We both talked seriously and laughed about it. It was always helpful for me to have my parents and friends who cared about me to talk these things through. It motivated me in a positive way to continue to do well in school and in my career opportunities to prove anyone wrong who might think that certain types of minorities may not be as strong performers, or simply successful due to affirmative action.

## MY THOUGHTS FOR PARENTS

*Read books such as* The Autobiography of an Ex-Colored Man *and others that talk about racial identity and how others have come into their own. Stay as positive as you can when having these discussions, so that no given race carries any negative connotation. The main point is to get your child thinking about his or her own racial identity, but be advised that this needs to come naturally as your child is living her life and being exposed to different people and media. Being a good human being is the most important goal in life, and this should be emphasized above all.*

*Another good exercise is to show your child photos and writings about different cultures—especially the ones pertaining to your child. Show your child articles and pictures of prominent Americans of various ethnicities who are professionals, artists, and even celebrities of similar racial makeup who are doing things that your family believes are positive: volunteering, contributing to the common good, caring for those who have less, or whatever matters in your family. These things reinforce the idea that people of all races make great contributions to the community and society, which provides a balance to the Eurocentric education your child will most probably receive in school.*

*This is easier said than done, as some media outlets and even regular people in society forcefully convey the message that black = bad, or black = poor, or black = thuggish, or black = people who don't speak proper English and are not as highly educated, or black = not as beautiful (I personally had to tackle this stereotype). As parents of a child of a different race you must reinforce early on both the fact that you are all a family no matter who is white or black or brown. Help your child to take pride in their ethnic makeup as something special and teach them about the corresponding cultures. Make sure you learn about important historic and current figures that your child can look up to. Know these things so you can bring them up in conversation. And make friends with people who look like your child.*

## GROWING INTO AN IDENTITY

Today, as a thirty-year-old lawyer, I personally identify most with my African American heritage and feel a connection in my soul to the history of struggles that African Americans in this country have faced. Beyond that, I identify myself with my multiracial ethnic makeup, being black, Japanese, and white, and having a "racially ambiguous" appearance. Mixed, if you will. There are a lot of mixed people out there these days, and I feel it is indicative of the melting pot that our country has become. I also love going overseas and having locals ask me if I am from that country, be it Indonesia, India, Brazil, or South Africa—in each place I can usually blend in more than my white counterparts, which can be fun!

Regarding my identity as an African American as a child, teen, and young adult, it was important for my parents to have me watch documentaries such as "Eyes on the Prize," and read books on the civil rights movement and slavery in America. My parents flooded me with information. School had so little information for me, but my parents gave me books, articles, and documentary television shows. In my eyes, black history was elevated to great importance in the makeup of our country—despite it being a few sentences in my school textbook. Reading books like *King Leopold's Ghost* (Hochschild, 1998) connected me to the racism and struggles in African colonization which fed into those in America.

I took my first trip to Ghana, Africa, when I was 14 years old, and that experience changed me—for the better. I went with 15 other teens to work both in the city of Accra and in the surrounding countryside. We worked with local pastors and children. Although my parents didn't come with me, they supported me in every way, from helping me raise the money to go to sending me with enough letters that I had something to open 5 days out of 7 (this was before the internet and cell phones—letters sent from home would have taken 3 weeks to arrive!). This was one of 9 trips I would make to Ghana which have included humanitarian aid, evangelism, teaching Bible studies, and building churches and community centers. I realized that there is a whole world outside of America, full of people who live differently than us and who are proud of their culture. And, I learned that even though I was from a different country, I could have a meaningful connection with the people I met over there. I learned that there are so many aspects of being a "human" that trump any issues of race. In addition, I learned that I was so very fortunate to have access to running water, healthy food, and an education, as much of the world struggles to obtain things we in America take for granted. It's amazing how many of the struggles and drama we deal with become much smaller in our minds when we are grateful for the things we do have and focus on that.

It was equally important to me to enroll in an African American literature class in college—that experience probably gave me more pride in my African American heritage than any other experience, because I read books like *Invisible Man* and *Diary of an Ex-Colored Man*, and connected with the expressed emotional turmoil and sense of pride that has gone with the experience of being black in America over the years. Reading this literature gave me a greater appreciation for how intensely volatile the issue of race is in America and why that is so. It was in taking this course, as well as an African American History course, that I really connected with the sense of what it means to be black in America and started to grapple with how it has set the stage for many of the economic and social issues that some African Americans face today.

Personally, I refer to myself as *both* black and brown any given day. My good friend who is Hispanic always calls herself a brown girl, and I also find that term endearing and fitting. But I am also proud to be an African American, "black," as well as a global citizen and a multi-cultural person. This latter part has come from years of traveling overseas to parts of Africa, South America, and Asia to engage in mission work, particularly with orphans and at-risk children living in poverty.

The other much more important factor in my gaining confidence in the way I look was, as I have mentioned elsewhere, the growing strength of my internal confidence in being a child of God. I no longer need to be complimented or noticed to feel valued—I know I'm already valued by the One whose opinion matters most. And that is the best feeling in the world.

## PERSPECTIVE FOR PARENTS: A FINAL WORD

I would like to put my whole experience of being an interracial adoptee in perspective, because even though the issue of race and being an interracial family is an important one, I would say that the preeminent issue has *not* been that of race and identity, but that of being adopted—given up for adoption by my biological mother (father was not in the picture) and reconciling that fact in my soul. Said another way, the preeminent "heart issue," if you will, for me, was overcoming a latent fear of abandonment. This issue which was not something I consciously lamented, but instead something that I struggled through with recurring dreams.

When I was a child, I would always have dreams that my parents were leaving me behind somewhere. In one dream, my parents and I were in an airport and they boarded a flight and left me at the airport. In another dream, my parents and I were in a boat, and I was put in another boat and they sailed off away from me. Even though I knew 100 percent that my parents loved me and would never leave me, I still had a latent subconscious issue of being left behind or rejected which would manifest in my dreams.

I would wake up from these dreams very saddened and scared. It was only through bringing these dreams to the attention of my parents, and talking them through and praying through the latent fears behind the dreams that I was having, that the haunting dreams ceased. One night my mom said "I wonder, honey, if you are having these dreams and they are really about your birth parents. Your mind has put our faces on your biological parents, because you don't remember the faces of your birth parents." We talked more and prayed together and I believe I received inner healing from a fear of abandonment that stemmed from my being given up for adoption, because I never had those dreams again.

*So my final advice for parents? Love your child, love all of who she is—her strengths and her growing edges. Learn about her cultural history and celebrate that as part of our greater American history. Be interested and be willing to combat those who would be happy to dismiss or diminish who your child is because of her race or her person. But above all, learn to be a family together—a family of people who may not look alike but are of one heart and mind.*

# NOTE

1. Hereinafter, my adoptive parents, who adopted me when I was a three-month-old baby, shall be solely referred to as my "parents," because that is what they are. I simply referred to them as such in the first instance for clarity's sake. My biological parents, whom I have never met, will be referred to as such.

# BIBLIOGRAPHY

Hochschild, A. (1998). *King Leopold's ghost: A story of greed, terror, and heroism in colonial Africa*. New York: Houghton Mifflin Co.

# CHAPTER 2

# I Never Thought about Race Growing Up

JANE HOYT-OLIVER

―――――――――――――――――――――――――――――――――――――――――――――――――――――――――――――――――――――――――――――――― ∽

*Just the other day our family walked into a large amusement park. My son looked around and then looked at me. "Mom, do you know why people are looking at us? It is because you are white." I loved that.*
Brandy, an adoptive mom of four boys
adopted transracially in Ohio

Why do families choose to adopt a child of a different race? What is it in their own lives that brought them to this decision? Were the topics of race and culture even part of their family's conversation? Does it matter whether adoptive parents have thought about race prior to their child entering the family? Do they have knowledge of deeper issues related to race that exist below the surface? These critical questions are examined in this chapter.

It is estimated that of the 1.7 million adoptions completed in the United States annually, approximately 40 percent could be defined as *transracial;* that is the adoptee is categorized as being of a race different than the adoptee's parent. Many of these transracial adoptions are *transnational adoptions*: parents adopting children from a country other than the United States. There has been a good amount of research exploring the joys and the concerns of this group of parents. But, there is another group of parents who adopt a child born within the United States. These are *transracial* adoptions. The vast majority of transracially adopting parents are racially categorized as Caucasian, although there are some families of color, such as African American families who adopt Caucasian children as well (Davenport, 2013). Many of these youngsters, first in foster care, have formed a loving and secure bond with their Caucasian parents.

## THE CHOICES WITHIN ADOPTION

Adoption can be a beautiful thing. It brings people together to form a family. It gives a child in need of permanent relationships a family for a lifetime while giving adoptive parents the opportunity to love and nurture another person. Each person in the family (including the adoptee) chooses to what extent to he or she will merge personal history, personality, and life understanding with the others in the family. These choices begin from the outset of the adoption experience and continue throughout the lives of the family members. Over time, these choices create a new family unit, which will have a unique culture, norms, and rules. In many cases, these choices resonate into the next generation as the stories family members tell their own children.

There are a myriad of choices within the context of adoption. Sometimes the choices are conscious and easy: for example, parents can choose to celebrate both the birthday and the "homecoming" day of an adoptive child as a way of celebrating the creation of a "forever family." But some choices are made because of the unconscious understandings about life that parents or children bring with them into the adoption. For example, adoptive parents may or may not choose to tell their child he is adopted. Or they might not choose to go deeper after the initial truth to sharing their life history with them. Adoptive children may believe that they must "be perfect" or their new parents will "send them back"; conversely, children may act out as a defense mechanism against the possibility of feeling loved because they assume the connection to their adoptive parents is temporary (Schooler, Smalley, & Callahan, 2010).

There is a great deal of good information available about issues that parents must discuss if they are adopting children. Some of the best books and blogs about adoption in general are included at the back of this volume in the "resources for adopting parents" section. But in *addition* to issues that arise during every adoption, research has shown that parents who adopt transracially face important issues that are not simply concerns about parenting style or separation from birth families (Quiroz, 2007).

Transracially adopting parents, their children, and their extended families (in some cases this extended network includes the biological parents of the adopted child) will deal with issues of race both within the context of their family and within the context of their communities. Although some have stated that we live in a "post racial" society, the lived experience of people of color and most transracially adopting families is that race is still very much an issue that their children confront on a daily basis (Smith, Juarez, & Jacobson, 2011). The authors of this book contend that we do not live in a post-racial society, but a *racialized* one (Kelly, Machery, & Mallon, 2012). Families who adopt transracially become conspicuous families, often simply because of the differing color of the family members' skin.

As Emerson and Smith noted, "Race is intimately tied to the American experience . . . a racialized society is a society wherein race matters profoundly for differences in life experiences, life opportunities, and social relationships" (2000, pp. 5–6). Neighbors and friends may say they "do not see color," but consciously or unconsciously, make assumptions about those they encounter based on stereotypical ideas. Those who parent children of color must develop skills to recognize prejudice and to confront such behaviors when they occur. They will want to protect their children from racism, but they also must prepare their children to find their place in a racialized world.

People do not come to parenthood as "blank slates"; they bring their history and their understanding of gender, race, culture, and traditions, as well as their hopes and dreams. They are aware consciously or subconsciously of the norms and expectations of the communities in which they reside. Parents who have already adopted transracially, and even those parents who are considering transracial adoption, should challenge themselves to consider how race is conceptualized by those who live in their communities. These important skills don't come naturally to many Caucasian parents. They were born and raised as members of the "preferred" racial group in the United States, and as such many have not had to consider race as an issue.

## PARENTS IN THE STUDY

How does one begin this journey as a transracially adoptive parent? It is best to begin with ourselves, and critically consider how we thought about race as children. If we can recognize how we understood race when we were growing up, we can more clearly conceive of how we can plan to address the issue of race within our families. If we can plan how to address the issues within our families, we can better prepare our children for a world that continues to stratify people along racial lines.

We asked parents who had adopted transracially to tell us about what they remembered about race when they were growing up. Our study focused on how parents who have adopted transracially understood the concept of race prior to the adoption of children and how the adoption of a child who is seen by society as being a different race had affected the parent's understanding of race. We were interested to learn if situations in their families of origin influenced their choice to adopt transracially, or if any experiences as adults had influenced this decision. We wanted to listen carefully to the stories the parents remembered about their lives growing up and we were curious to know if we could uncover common themes in the lives of these parents that had assisted them to make this choice. As Atkinson notes, "Stories [play] a central role in the lives of . . . people. . . . It [is] through [stories] that the timeless elements of life are transmitted" (Atkinson, 2001).

We interviewed transracially adopting couples in committed relationships. The couples resided in Massachusetts, Ohio, and Pennsylvania. Eleven of the 13 couples were heterosexual and were married; two were same sex couples in long term-committed relationships. The couples were parents to 27 transracially adopted children. Interviews took place over a period of eight months.

Participants ranged from 36 to 73 years when they were interviewed. They had adopted between one and seven children; although most had adopted either one or two children.

Many of the parents we interviewed were "typical" of many parents who elect to adopt. A number of the couples had attempted to become pregnant without success, and then turned to adoption as a way to expand their family. One mother commented:

*We started in foster care simply because when we went to that first meeting they basically said because we were there to adopt and [the county social worker] said, "Good luck . . . if you aren't willing to foster first you might as well be ready to wait about six years." I will never forget her saying that.*

A few couples had talked about adoption early in their relationship and had agreed together that if it was possible they would like to adopt transracially. One couple spoke of a professor who had mentored the couple during their college years. This professor had adopted a child from each continent. His example had been the catalyst for their decision to try to adopt transracially. Others seem to have made the decision as a way to balance the structural inequality that they observed in the United States.

One father commented:

*I felt I had a bond with the black community more than the average white person. I wanted to do my part and I thought this could be a kind of sweet thing to do, to, have a mixture of races in the family. I wanted to try to do my part to reject the imbalance.*

## THE PREPARATION OF ADOPTIVE PARENTS: ARE PARENTS ASKED THE RIGHT QUESTIONS?

Adoption may not always be the *first* choice that a couple might pursue when deciding to expand their family, but it *is a choice*. Adopting couples choose to become parents, and are evaluated by social workers with specialized adoption training. The process is often long and costly. The parents' "suitability" is evaluated and their motives for becoming parents are discussed. Professionals come to their home, speak to them about their background, their growing up, their current relationships, and so on. Even though the process has become more transparent in the past few decades, it often feels invasive. Adopting parents must discuss issues that birth parents may not have discussed before the birth of their child.

Adoption is a privilege that is bound by the hopes, dreams, and loves of potential parents as well as by the laws and rules of the states in which the couples reside. Most parents take these issues seriously and spend hours discussing them together. But what happens when no one asks the potential transracially adoptive parents the right questions. What happens if they don't know about or don't believe that issues of racism exist which will impact their family? Why would this be the case? The rest of this chapter explores two critical issues that are below the surface: *unconscious privilege* and *structural racism* and how important it is for transracially adoptive parents to grow in awareness and understanding.

## UNCONSCIOUS PRIVILEGE: "I NEVER THOUGHT ABOUT RACE GROWING UP"

When we asked the parents in our study to think back and remember what they thought about race when they were young, many indicated that they had not thought about race as children. Most were born and raised in predominantly white communities. The following represent the recollections of a number of participants.

> *I think that growing up, I didn't think about race. I grew up in a community that was very white. . . . I didn't see a child of color in school with me until I was in high school. And there was not a lot of understanding and acceptance of difference. Certainly not to any level of appreciation.*
>
> *I grew up in a pretty white suburban town. I remember that in high school was when I had the first black classmate of mine. It just wasn't the world that we were exposed to.*
>
> *I didn't think of anything about [race and culture] because there were not African Americans around us. Everything was white. It was just an all-white culture and you didn't talk about it.*
>
> *I grew up in a time where communities were very segregated in the northeast. When I was young we moved to a truly segregated community where blacks weren't allowed to buy homes.*

These parents grew up in communities with very little racial diversity. As children, racial issues were rarely a topic of family conversation People who were identified as coming from a different race were to be seen at best as "different" from the members of the community, and at worst, a threat to the community itself.

## STRUCTURAL RACISM

Although many parents did not consciously discuss race within their home communities, several did have experiences in which they were confronted with structural racism. In some cases, these encounters became organizing events in their lives and led to questioning. For example, one woman reported:

> *In the community in which I grew up an African American family came to town to look at a house. I will never forget it. There were men from the town that actually stoned their car. These people literally could not get out of their car to, to get out to the house. I'll never forget it— EVER! I was ashamed to be from there. I remember it so clearly. I can't even tell you why I was so affected by it. But I really was. It was awful.*

In other cases, the situations became events by which the participants perceived structural injustice, but were unsure how to address the observed injustices. Rather than taking on the observed structural oppression (perhaps a tall order when one is young and thus relatively powerless), some participants resolved to change themselves.

*My story started when I was in fifth grade and we did a project. I grew up in a very small, white town. When I was in high school, the only black man in my community was married to a white woman and they had a biracial son. I remember him saying that he was going to move out of town before his child would enter school. . . .*

*At the end of the project the teacher said, now, how many of you would help somebody out of the ghetto if you had a chance? And I was the only one in the class that said yes.*

The statements of the parents above reflect a widely held belief that individual insight and effort can change the community. By adopting transracially, these parents believe they are a part of creating a more inclusive world family by family. There is clearly truth to this idea, but it is also important to make sure that as the world is changing, parents support their children in the world that currently exists as well.

## THE CONSEQUENCES OF A LACK OF AWARENESS

What are the potential consequences when growing up in a community where diversity wasn't experienced? Often people do not learn the skills needed to critically examine issues of race in their families; indeed, in many families, race may not have been considered important to discuss. Thus, transracially adopting parents may not know where to begin to develop the skills needed to guide their children of color successfully. Having not talked about race in their childhoods, they may miss cues to their children's experiences in their communities, especially as the children become adolescents. For example, are the children unwilling to walk to the store because they are "being lazy teenagers," or is it because they are being taunted by others in the neighborhood or followed by law enforcement when they are walking without their parents?

## EXPERIENCING DIVERSITY: THE CONTRAST IN UNDERSTANDING

In contrast to the parents in our study who had little or no contact with children of color in their formative years, a few parents in the study had significant experiences in their childhoods which made the possibility of transracial adoption seem not only feasible but *normative*; for example:

> *In my growing up years, we had about 70 or 80 foster kids in our home, a few of them racially mixed. We were privileged to begin our family with an adopted son who was biracial. The social workers would call and say, "You're already mixed up anyway, so would you consider another one?"*

In this parent's situation, social workers assisting with the adoption knew that the parent had experience with interracial family groupings and thus were more willing to place a biracial child with the couple. Once the initial placement was "working well," the family was cleared to parent additional children who were biracial or African American. The social workers assumed that this large "multiracial" family would provide a supportive environment for the children.

## KEY FIRST STEPS FOR TRANSRACIALLY ADOPTING PARENTS

Parents who plan to adopt transracially need to be aware not only of their own understanding of the place that race continues to play in the United States, but be aware of how race is perceived by others. Part of a parent's task is to prepare children for the world that they will enter as adults. None of us can do that completely, but we can dedicate ourselves to learning what we need to know to assist in that process. The discussion below is provided so that parents can strengthen their awareness of how race is currently conceptualized in the United States.

## PARENTING AND WHITE PRIVILEGE

Scholarly definitions of race in the 19th and 20th centuries often reflected an understanding of race that seemed absolute. The 1994 edition of *Webster's New Universal Unabridged Dictionary* contained several definitions for *race*, including; "(1) a group of people related by common descent, blood, or heredity. . . .; (5) the condition of belonging to a certain ethnic stock; (6) the distinguishing characteristics of various ethnic stocks" (p. 1184). It was assumed that people could be categorized by their racial characteristics. In the late 1800s and early 20th century, many social scientists studied people of what were then considered "different races" and published scholarly work that often reflected racial stereotypes that were common during those centuries. During this time, the assumption by many in the academic community was that the strongest or most dominant race was what was then called "Caucasian": those who were descendants of people who, it was believed at that time, had originated in Mesopotamia and what is now Europe.

Although this definition can still be found in current dictionaries, there is often an extended caveat to these definitions. One such caveat introduces the concept that race is not biologically based but is a socially created concept. This was noted on freedictionary.com in 2014.

*The notion of race is nearly as problematic from a scientific point of view as it is from a social one. European physical anthropologists of the 17th and 18th centuries proposed various systems of racial classifications based on such observable characteristics as skin color, hair type, body proportions, and skull measurements, essentially codifying the perceived differences among broad geographic populations of humans. The traditional terms for these populations—Caucasoid (or Caucasian), Mongoloid, Negroid, and in some systems Australoid—are now controversial in both technical and nontechnical usage, and in some cases they may well be considered offensive. (Caucasian does retain a certain currency in American English, but it is used almost exclusively to mean "white" or "European" rather than "belonging to the Caucasian race," a group that includes a variety of peoples generally categorized as nonwhite.) The biological aspect of race is described today not in observable physical features but rather in such genetic characteristics as blood groups and metabolic processes, and the groupings indicated by these factors seldom coincide very neatly with those put forward by earlier physical anthropologists. Citing this and other points—such as the fact that a person who is considered black in one society might be nonblack in another—* many cultural anthropologists now consider race to be more a social or mental construct than an objective biological fact. *[Emphasis added]*

Many social scientists now claim that although race continues to be a very important concept in the United States, it is *a socially constructed* concept: that groups assign characteristics to individuals based not on the *reality* of racial/ biological characteristics, but on what the more powerful groups in society have stereotypically *assigned to the group* as group characteristics. These assignments have both conscious and unconscious consequences for all members of society.

In the United States, a country in which the descendants of Europeans have significant influence and power, these assignments have led to interpretations of history that ignore important contributions by non-Caucasian groups (e.g., ignoring the extent to which the economic contributions of enslaved Africans assisted the overall development of Northern colonies before the American revolution) and the way in which the majority culture named important actions in the country's past (e.g., did hardy pioneers "tame the west" or inflict literal or cultural genocide on Native Americans?). This social narrative can have far reaching effects for all citizens, both those who benefited from the myths and those who have not.

Some effects we can easily see. When we are taught that the most important inventions and ideas have been formulated by those of European descent, it reinforces the idea that whites are on average more capable than other groups. But often what we are taught is incomplete. Few high school texts provide information on those free and enslaved people who fought for freedom in the American Revolution or about the important inventions created by citizens of color such as stoplights or a way to store and transfuse blood. Such information provides a more complete picture of the contributions that people of color made to the economic and cultural development of the country. The information can be obtained at the high school level by taking courses in "African American History" or other specialized courses that focus on specific groups. That implies that this history must be kept separate from "American History," which has traditionally focused on the accomplishments of those of European descent. In many states a course in African American History is not required in high school. Thus, most adults in the United States have an incomplete picture of those who built the country and of the sacrifices and choices that we made in its forming. The majority develops an incomplete understanding of those around us, and that can lead to inaccurate judgments based on conscious or unconscious stereotypes.

This leads to a discussion of another important idea that is not often mentioned in mainstream culture, the concept of *white privilege*. This term encompasses many different ideas, but the overarching idea is that there is a structural advantage to being considered white in the

United States. Because of the incomplete picture of society, people of European descent have been able to claim advantages which include; access to the majority of inherited wealth, the reality that people of European descent created laws (where people of color could live, go to school or be buried) and norms (quotas on the number of people of color allowed into the country's most prestigious schools and universities) that, up until a generation ago it was more difficult, if not impossible for people of color to access society's benefits. Most scholars accept this as a true reflection of social structure in the United States even as they acknowledge that most whites remain unaware of the privileges that have been granted to them.

As educators Dunbar, Rodriguez, and Parker wrote, "In the contemporary context of American and Western society, being 'white' is the unreflected upon standard from which all other racial identities vary" (Dunbar, Rodriguez, & Parker, 2001). As noted earlier, for the many parents in our study who had grown up in predominantly white communities, race was rarely discussed and the concept of white privilege was not understood or accepted. When one has been raised within the dominant culture, the unconscious privilege of that culture is, in one sense an inherited, but unasked for, gift passed from one generation to the next. Schmitz (2010) notes, "the journey to an awareness of white privilege is messy, imperfect, disconcerting and lifelong" (p. 15). Parents from our study clearly grappled with these issues: both within themselves and with their children, as well as within the communities in which they live.

Many parents in our study were unaware of how "whiteness" is normalized, or of the privileges and powers that are afforded to them by society based on their race. Some parents were aware of events of racism that had been directed at members of the communities in which they grew up. However, when those events were life altering, for most of the parents we spoke to, a transformative change of their worldview was *a choice*. The woman who told the story about the African American family who was not allowed to get out of their car was not the only child who observed this terrible incident that day, but she may have been one of the only people in the community for whom the incident was life-changing. How many other children from the community witnessed this incident and did not think too much more about it? Observing the story from another perspective, we can imagine that the children of the family *in the car* remembered the incident, and could have easily passed the story of the town's intolerance down to their own children.

Like the people in the car, children identified by society as children of color are not afforded the choice to be perceived as a person of color. Parents who adopt transracially need to hold onto this reality as they parent their children, and to be aware that they live in a world in which the realities of privilege intersect with the potential lessened privilege for their children.

Educator and transracially adopting mother Martha Satz (1992) eloquently wrote, "With great trepidation I articulate what I think to be true . . . my own racial identity has shifted. I am not now, of course, a woman of color outwardly . . . but my consciousness has shifted inalterably. I have experienced racism, not first-hand . . . but in its closest approximation" (p. 8). That the essay goes on to argue against transracial adoption as yet another example of the "egotistical trap of white privilege—valuing my own advantages over the societal good" (p. 11) shows how very complex this issue remains.

Parents who adopt transracially will confront such complexities time and time again. Caucasian parents who adopt transracially should not assume that their community will embrace and protect their children simply because *the parents* have not encountered prejudice in the past. As discussed later in the book, parents raising transracial children may experience initial acceptance of their children as infants, but find decreasing acceptance as the child grows. The pervasive history of racism in the United States impacts every community, and it is sometimes quite overt (e.g., the many examples of being followed by security personnel in stores, or being followed by police), but can often be very subtle (being overlooked by a salesperson for the white person who is standing behind you in line).

What many parents discover is that "simply" loving their adopted children does not change the reality of structural racism in the lives of their children. They cannot protect their children from the world, as protection extends only so far. Children grow up not only in our families but in schools and community institutions. Although parents' words have the initial ability to shape a good deal of a child's understanding of who he or she is, the members of the community may attempt to limit the child's life chances based on racialized community norms. This was brought home vividly to one of the authors of this book several years ago while visiting with friends from college. She was boasting about her (of course, *amazing*) daughter, when one person causally remarked "She sounds wonderful. It's really too bad that her opportunities will be so limited because she's biracial."

Perhaps such comments are bound by the time (the early 1990s) or by the circumstances (how the couple saw the "more conservative" world they lived in as opposed to the "more liberal" world in which the author resided). But the comment was also an important one for the author, for she knew at that moment that her parental desire that her daughter would seamlessly fit into whatever community the daughter chose to live in could be hampered by something that was simply out of her control: how the community viewed her as a biracial woman.

This, of course, does not mean that transracially adopting parents simply acknowledge our racialized society, as well as the privilege that comes from being born into the majority culture. Parenting transracially places them in a place between cultural norms, and may, in fact, be challenging to those norms. Parents must first prepare themselves by understanding the realities of racism in the United States.

## PREPARING FOR THE REALITIES

How can this be done? How can parents move away from the accepted understanding of "how the world works" and into a richer more complex understanding of life in the United States?

- Read books, magazines and blogs
- Talk to friends
- Ask questions that, in the past, you might not have thought to ask
- Assume that you are not the expert on such issues

One participant in our study, the father of two children, one who had been adopted when the child was in elementary school, believed that the adoption meant that every member of the family needed to adjust to the new "family" culture. He noted:

*The adoption forced us to really engage in conversations with other people—to move away from some friends, develop much closer alliances with others, and to make sure we were rooted in a religious community that was reflective and supportive of our family. We have taken our responsibility pretty seriously and it's enriched our lives in ways that are beyond measure.*

Parents can create room in the family for discussions about race and racism. Sometimes these can be held in "family meeting" times, but often the discussions come up when everyday events occur at home or in the news. As we write this book, for example, the newspaper reports that the FBI is investigating who might have placed a noose around the statue of James Meredith, the man who integrated the University of Mississippi in the 1960s. Transracial families could use this event to discuss the courage of Mr. Meredith, as well as the ongoing and painful personal toll his choice extracted on his life. Some will most likely see this incident as a "harmless prank" and others will see it as much more. Either way, it can be transformed into a teachable moment between parent and child. These discussions alert children that the parents are open to talking about this painful issue. With the help of knowledgeable community allies (social workers, friends who are of the same racial group as the child), as a family create strategies to deal with discrimination as it occurs. It is important to assume that it will occur.

Every parent in our study indicated that they had identified parental responsibilities related to race and culture. All but two of the participants had talked with their child about race and prejudice, and over 80 percent had spoken with an adult of their child's race about coping with prejudice. Three-quarters of the participants had discussed "a few coping strategies to deal with race-based teasing" with their children. The deeper question here was whether the strategies that had been discussed had helped the child to cope with the issues that had arisen. When asked about specific strategies, one mother answered:

> *I don't know where to begin. I've done some reading and issues of race will definitely continue as my daughter dates and goes to high school. We're thinking of strategies for high school. We're thinking of private school: not that it won't come up there, but it might come up differently. I don't know, I think it will come up wherever we are.*

The mom is concerned about issues that arise because of the child's race. On one hand, she acknowledges that these issues will definitely continue. She has consulted with friends who also have adopted transracially, and their experience has been that issues about race increase as children mature and get older. She clearly is interested in shielding her child from the pain of racism, is considering sending the child to a private rather than a public school (a strategy historically used as a protective measure by parents of privilege), but acknowledges that this may not shield her child from hurt. It may be that she feels she will be better able to control the racism when it does occur: as a parent who is paying for education, the assumption is that the administration may be more open to addressing such concerns.

This parent was also in a group of adopting parents, but not all of these parents had adopted transracially. Later in the interview, she spoke of how difficult the next few years might be as her daughter moves into adolescence. This mom hoped that the hard work that she is doing now will provide the family with resilience as her daughter begins to differentiate herself as an African American woman.

> *I guess we'll be doing more leaning on [my parenting group]. There's talk about finding mentors for the children. I anticipate my daughter may be critical; that'll be her job anyway. I expect some of it might be focused on race. She might question why she has to be in a white family. She might get mad at us. One of my friends asked if we were afraid if she will turn on us when she's a teenager. It's an on-going conversation about our transracial family and what people think, how a girl is supposed to think and look and act. It is the whole social class thing.*

## HOW CAN WE LEARN WHAT WE NEED TO KNOW? CHARTING NEW PATHS

No one who becomes a parent knows everything. In previous generations, families might have relied on the extended family for wisdom. In the 21st century, many young couples do not live close to their families, and even with e-mail, Skype, and other technological advances, "hands on" wisdom is harder to come by. Some of the questions that might be answered by parents or older siblings about parenting children if the parents and the children were identified as the same race, may not be as applicable when it comes to asking questions about how to deal with discrimination.

Not only do most family members lack the life experience to assist the adopting couples, often the extended family members in our study were perceived by the couples as ambivalent or hostile to the adoption. This is an issue that generations of adopting parents have struggled with, even those who adopted in-racially, but parents in our study more often than not perceived that the extended family focused their disapproval not on the *adoption itself*, but the fact that the adoption *was transracial*. For example:

*My mother-in-law was not happy. She said, you can be friends with them, but you don't bring them in your house. It became that I was the bad one. So you know when my mother-in-law tells this joke and it uses the N-word. It's inappropriate in a circle in our family when you're trying to get a laugh because of the word. Nobody said anything. I addressed it, and nothing was done. We had talked about it before we went, because I knew it would come up again. If we didn't set the boundary and say this is unacceptable that it would happen again.*

Parents who plan to adopt transracially need to think about the impact that the adoption will have on extended family dynamics. Having these conversations can be very difficult. At the end of this chapter are questions that can be used in a family setting or in a support group setting to further explore the issues challenging transracially adoptive families.

There are many additional questions that might be helpful to discuss. Know, of course, that one can never anticipate every question, but beginning with some of these very basic ones can provide an important beginning.

## SUMMARY

Transracially adopting parents, their children, and their extended families, will deal with issues of race both within the context of their family and within the context of their communities. There are many things to consider.

1. Many parents in our study who adopted transracially did not think about race when growing up.
2. There are consequences to a lack of examination or lack of awareness regarding racial issues. Such life experiences lead to a lack of understanding regarding the reality of white privilege and structural racism.
3. Parents who have already adopted transracially and even those parents who are considering transracial adoption are challenged to think about how race is conceptualized by those who live in their communities.
4. There are a number of things parents can do to prepare for the reality of what their child's experiences will be. These include becoming a student of your child's life experiences by starting conversations, by asking good questions, and by creating a

healthy communicative environment in the home where conversations around difficult issues can readily be shared.

## QUESTIONS FOR SUPPORT GROUPS

Preparing to discuss the issue takes forethought. Here are a few questions that couples might consider discussing before they meet with other family members:

1. How does the extended family deal with other difficult issues? Do they deal with them at all?
2. Will adult extended family members support or isolate the couple's adopted children from cousins and other children close in age to the adopted child?
3. Who will take responsibility to call family members on remarks or actions that are hurtful to the adoptive child and adoptive family?
4. Who will take responsibility to correct the younger children in the extended family if those children say or act in a way that would be hurtful to the adopted child and adoptive family?
5. Think about the ways in which people of a different race have been discussed in other family settings in the past.
6. What does each member of the couple anticipate may be concerns or objections that might be raised by the extended family?
7. Who will take the "lead" if painful issues arise? For example, will the wife take the lead in discussing issues with her family and the husband take the lead with his?
8. After the adoption, who will take the lead on other issues that may arise? Can the family agree in advance to allow the couple (or the adopted child him/herself!) to express concern if a remark or action is perceived as racist?

There are many additional questions that might be helpful to discuss. Know, of course, that one can never anticipate every question, but some of these very basic ones can provide an important beginning.

## BIBLIOGRAPHY

Atkinson, R. (2001). The life story interview. In J. F. Gubrium & J. A. Holstein (Eds.), *Handbook of interview research*. Thousand Oaks, CA: Sage Publications.

Davenport, D. (2013). Transracial adoption twist: African American parents adopting white kids. *Creating a family*. Retrieved from http://www.creatingafamily.org/blog/transracial-adoption-twist-black-parents-adopting-white-kids/

Dunbar Jr., C., Rodriguez, D., & Parker, L. (2001). Race, subjectivity, and the interview process. In J. F. Gubrium & J. A. Holstein (Eds.), *Handbook of interview research*. Thousand Oaks, CA: Sage Publications.

Emerson, M. O., & Smith, C. (2000). *Divided by faith: Evangelical religion and the problem of race in America*. New York: Oxford University Press.

Free Dictionary. (2014). Race. *Thefreedictionary.com*.

Kelly, D., Machery, E., & Mallon, R. (2012). Race and racial cognition. In J. Doris (Ed.), *The moral psychology handbook*. Oxford, U.K.: Oxford University Press.

Merriam Webster, Inc. (1994). Race. In *Webster's new universal unabridged dictionary* (p. 1184). New York: Random House.

Quiroz, P. A. (2007). *Adoption in a color-blind society*. Lanham, MD: Rowman & Littlefield Publishers.

Satz, M. (1992). Transracial mothering: Double-edged privilege. *Journal of Social Distress and the Homeless, 17*(1/2), 8–36.

Schmitz, D. S. (2010). Developing an awareness of white privilege. *Reflections: Narratives of Professional Helping, 16*(1), 15–20.

Schooler, J. E., Smalley B. K., & Callahan, T. J. (2010). *Wounded children, healing homes: How traumatized children impact adoptive and foster families*. Colorado Springs, CO: Nav Press, Inc.

Smith, D. T., Juarez, B. G., & Jacobson, C. K. (2011). White on black: Can white parents teach black adoptive children how to understand and cope with racism? *Journal of Black Studies, 42*(8), 1195–1230.

# CHAPTER 3

# Dealing with Race in the Extended Family and Community

## JANE HOYT-OLIVER

> *From one part of our family, we had a very angry reaction that was heartbreaking. WE were just ecstatic about our first baby. He was beautiful in our totally objective opinion. I could hardly stop smiling for about a month. But there were some folks close to us in the family who got angry and said, "if that's the way it is going to be, don't ever come home again."*

Adopting transracially doesn't just touch the lives of the adoptive parents and child, but has an impact on family and community as well. The meaning of what was once called the adoption triad (child, birth parents, and adoptive parents) has evolved into something that encompasses much more. Author Michael Grand first coined the phrase "adoption constellation" in 1994: the phrase broadens our understanding of who is affected by adoption and thus is affected by transracial adoption. The term adoption constellation "allows for the consideration of adoptees, birth parents and adoptive parents, but also incorporates birth and adoptive families, service providers, teachers, physicians, the courts, social service workers, legislators and the clergy. In fact, anyone whose life is entwined with adoption is a member of the constellation" (Grand, 2011). When adoptive parents choose to adopt transracially, their choice requires them to be open to the unique needs their child will have in relationship to extended family, neighborhood, community, and school.

Adopting parents sometimes take on the burden of re-educating their extended families, and in doing so they may need to be proactive about what will be acceptable or not acceptable when talking about and interacting with the couple's children. Parents need to assist their extended family members agree upon a set of rules based on standards of respect for all. At minimum, adoptive parents should decide together what is acceptable behavior and what is not acceptable: this mirrors a universal parental obligation. Just as parents agree that a child should be shielded from an extended family member who may be violent, or who has a history of abusive actions towards others, parents who adopt transracially should decide how they would protect their children from extended family members who hold racist beliefs, and must be proactive if these beliefs are expressed.

As noted in the previous chapter, people who have lived within the reality of white privilege often are unaware of how often society provides default benefits to them as members of the dominant racial group. When the concept is initially discussed, often privileged people justify their actions as harmless, and the person who is raising the concern as "too sensitive." This fits into the worldview of those who have not examined the ongoing state of racism in the United States. As Michael Emerson and Christian Smith wrote in their book *Divided by Faith* (2000), "the problems of race and the racial hierarchy have not disappeared at all. The forms have changed . . . leading us to the mistaken [conclusion that] racism is on the wane. . . . [Racial] practices that reproduce racial divisions in the contemporary United States (1) are increasingly covert, (2) are increasingly embedded in the normal operations of institutions, (3) avoid direct terminology, and (4) are invisible to most whites" (p. 9). Since many family members of the dominant culture are unaware that they are privileged, this will not be a "once and done" conversation, but part of the evolution of family conversations over time.

## CONVERSATIONS WITHIN THE FAMILY

Remarks made by family members, with or without malicious intent, may still reflect the unconscious belief that adopted children are "different." For example, an extended family member remarked to one of our authors that the author's child must enjoy swimming and diving because the child's birth grandparents had been citizens of an island nation. The assumption that the child's biological heritage would trump the reality that her birth parents also loved water sports seemed to the child's parents to point to the "otherness" of the adopted child. The conversation that followed between the parents and the family member was important to all involved. Taking the time and having the courage to talk about what is helpful and what might be harmful is critical to the developing story of the adopting family. The good news is, when adopting parents are clear about what they expect from their extended families, adoptive parents often find that initial negative reactions to their discussion about children from extended family members will change if challenged. For example, one parent noted:

> *You know if you had to choose your family, your new family, over cousins and aunts and uncles, you would. It's gotten to that point where we just went, o.k., if we ever get to the point where we're going to have to choose one or the other, we're just going to have to walk away from this. But luckily, thankfully, they're making an effort.*

## LEARNING TO THINK ABOUT RACE WITHIN THE CONTEXT OF COMMUNITY

Just over half of the families interviewed lived in neighborhoods where at least some of the neighbors reflect the child's race and described the communities where they lived as "very welcoming" to their transracial family. An additional third believed that their community had been "somewhat welcoming" to their family.

For families who live on the coasts, or in major cities, finding a community that is diverse is sometimes easier than for those living in the central part of the country. Research completed in 2012 which examined 2010 census data found that racial diversity is increasing in major cities across the United States, but that highly diverse neighborhoods are still rare (Barber, 2012). When parents can choose (and we know that some cannot), most opt to move to a neighborhood that is safe, where schools are good, and that is close to work. In some areas of the country, however, these neighborhoods and the institutions that surround them (e.g., schools, places of worship, members of the police and fire departments) may be very homogeneous.

Several families addressed concerns about the lack of diversity within their neighborhoods, as well as their struggle to balance the desire to be inclusive with the perceived realities of race/class divides. Some parents clearly struggle to balance the expressed needs of their children with their concern to protect and nurture their children. For example, one parent noted that the community in which he lives is predominantly white with many of the neighbors being either older or childless. His children want to be friends with those they meet in school, but many of those children live in impoverished neighborhoods in the surrounding community. His children often ask him if they can go down to their friends' neighborhood. He noted:

*I don't want you to feel like I am ill-tempered or anything, but I'm not going to drop an eight-year-old child at the housing project and say, "have a nice day."*

Later, he spoke about the ways in which he felt he and the children were left out of a number of the routine ways that social structures are reinforced in middle and upper middle class households.

*We have driven hundreds of kids, dozens of kids, hundreds of times . . . hundreds of thousands of round trips of other kids to soccer practice or basketball practice or whatever. You know, nobody else gives our kids rides.*

The situation described above is echoed by any number of families who adopt transracially. Even knowing that people of different races are treated differently within the United States, many transracially adopting Caucasian parents nonetheless begin their parenting believing that their children will *be treated as white* because the children are living with white parents. It seems as if the parents thought that they could "transfer their (white) privilege" to their children by socializing the children to the privileged world. For many, the numerous ways that their children are not included is both surprising and painful. The family unit can be warm, supportive, and loving, but the larger community, including the parents of the teens mentioned above, easily ignore the *quid pro quo* of shared rides so often a sign of community solidarity among middle class families.

When parents have grown up in communities with so little diversity that race was never discussed, having one or two people of color in one's community, school, or church may feel like "diversity." For their children, however, it may feel overwhelmingly monochromatic. One young man moved to a community that was overwhelmingly white when he was a teen because his father had changed jobs. The parents talked openly about their lack of choices regarding housing and continued to check in with the child about his adjustment throughout the year. About six months after the move, they discovered that one of the ways their child was coping was to mentally make an "unduplicated count" of the African American individuals he saw in the community (reportedly after six months the number was in the low two digits). They asked if they could join in the count. This became a point of family solidarity and a way to affirm that the entire family was missing the diverse community from which they had moved. Parents who adopt transracially understand that there are additional concerns for their multiracial family and many learn to address the issues with their children and community with wisdom and courage. These issues and how to address them will be discussed in the following chapters.

## TALKING ABOUT RACE WITH AN ADOPTED CHILD

All parents spend a good deal of time preparing their children for adulthood. Some of this occurs in the somewhat unconscious ebb and flow of everyday life, and some occurs when parents utilize teachable moments to interpret the world with their children. For parents who adopt transracially, this can be a complicated process. Even within the life of a family in which members are biologically related, interpretation of events within the life of the child can conflict with the understanding of the same event for the parent. Because the structures of society in the United States are governed by rules created by and structured around the norms and mores of Caucasian middle class ideals (Payne, DeVol, & Dreussi Smith, 2006) and their children of color do not conform to the norm of whiteness (Quiroz, 2007), the opportunity for miscommunication and possible alienation between parents and children can be heightened. For example, one parent in our study noted:

> *I try to say to my son, "You know, let's think, let's try to look at the other side a little bit and walk a few feet at least in the other guy's shoes." And he hears you're on the side of the KKK, so it's a struggle. Because I do want to teach my kids to think carefully and not to be a racist thinker, but you have to be very careful when you're bringing up kids.*

Another parent underscored her understanding of the importance of having a discussion about race, but also seemed unsure when it would be best to begin those discussions, even though her child had experienced negative racial situations in daycare. She stated:

*We will role play some of the things that come up we will deal with. I just think, she will be 4 soon. I don't know if at four I'm going to feel comfortable sitting down to discuss race and racism. I've read part of the Martin Luther King book to her, but I've kind of skipped over the part where the kid said, "I don't want to be your friend" or "we can't play with you anymore." At 11 they said, "we can't play with you anymore." I suppose if I was to read that now, I would do that because I know she's heard that also. And I feel bad as a mom.*

Another added:

*It makes me worry about what my children have to deal with. It makes me sad, that people will sometimes just look at them on the outside and judge them and not see who they are on the inside. And how else has it changed me? I think it made me more open to develop friendships and probably invite people over to the house. Maybe before I might have just said, "oh yeah, great to see you" or whatever. But now maybe I might say, "hey, you want to come over?"*

It is clear that the parents we interviewed loved their children; and it needs to be noted that parenting is challenging. But raising a child who is identified by society as belonging to a different race can bring unique challenges to families: even if the parents, as some parents alleged, "don't see race" when they look at their children, society clearly continues to do so. Even though a good number of research studies find few differences between children adopted transracially and those adopted interracially, the reality of navigating a world where race must at some level always be a consideration means that parents who have been brought up within the privileged world of whiteness must acquire the skills to assist their children to navigate a still racialized society. How parents handle these issues with their children, if they handle them, is of critical importance to the transracial family as a whole, to the parents, and, we believe, to the children.

Having received unearned privilege, but having few words with which to describe the structural racism that continues to bedevil our communities, the issues and concerns that transracially adopting parents face are met with strategies that often address the specific concern, but may not get to underlying issues. One parent noted:

*One time my daughter told me a story of something that happened in class. I went to talk to the teacher about it because she had a bruise and a cut on her shoulder. And the teacher said, "Oh, that didn't happen. I would have been aware of it had it happened." And I said, "OK. My daughter said some kid pushed her down and another boy helped her up." Well, by the time she told me, it had already been like hours. I mean, it had been the next day before I could've called the other little boy's mom to see what had happened. I just feel like the timing hasn't been right. I've been praying about it, that the stuff would come out that needed to come out. But her teacher said, "Oh, that didn't happen." I made my daughter apologize to the teacher and talked to her about what a lie was. And so she came home to me and she said, "So, Mom, if this really happened, if somebody did this to me, and I tell you it happened, then that's really right, Mom. And then if somebody else says it didn't, then that would be a lie, right?" And I said, "yeah." And she said, "well, then my teacher owes me an apology." . . . And you can't expect a three-year-old to stand up to a woman who's been teaching for 30 years.*

When the child's parent spoke to the teacher, the teacher insisted that the child was lying. The parent was then faced with a choice: does the parent punish her child on the basis of the teacher's report, or push the issue further on the basis of the child's report? For parents brought up within the comforts of white privilege, the assumption is often that the teacher would not miss such an important issue as a playground fight, because she is watching over the children; thus, Mom believed the teacher. Parents of color, however, having lived for generations with the petty aggressions of racism, might have asked more questions of both the child and the teacher, even risking being seen as "disrespectful" of that teacher by choosing to believe their child over the report of the teacher.

If parents have no true understanding of the structural underpinnings to racism, they will often attempt to find solutions that fit the individual situation in which they find themselves or that their children experience. They discuss these solutions with their children. One parent recalled:

*It's made me more aware of the need to get out there and provide opportunities for myself where I am the minority and where my children are the majority. We go once a week usually pretty much all year long, up to a branch of the library where the kids are in an environment where there are just a few of us Caucasian people. Everybody else is, um, African American.*

Over 90 percent of parents in our study agreed that they would "need to teach their children a variety of coping strategies from which to choose when faced with prejudice or bias." The question may be, however, do parents who grew up in a world that was structured around the needs and concerns of the Caucasian majority have these skills in their toolbox? Are they aware that they may need them? Are there ways in which parents might prepare themselves for the hard questions that arise for children of color in a world that continues to be anything but postracial?

Schmitz writes that privileged people, even those who desire to see justice come about can get caught in an attempt to protect themselves from the emotional pain that occurs when the reality of privilege is internalized. She notes, "My expectation of daily safeness highlights the privilege I constantly experience that often differs from the experiences of people of color" (Schmitz, 2010). It is clear then that parents who adopt transracially need to develop an additional skill set which will provide them with the ability to discuss and strengthen their children for the reality of racism that the children will encounter. Some of these skills can be learned through training, through friendships, within places of worship, and within community institutions that are known for addressing issues of race in a forthright manner and through study. For example, parents who attend a place of worship regularly may wish to discuss with the leaders of their faith community ways in which the church, synagogue, or mosque could assist adopting parents in this vital work.

Transracially adopting parents need to face unpleasant truths about racism courageously. This issue could be critical to their children's self-esteem. Talking courageously strengthens the ability of children to navigate the world as they mature. Many of these critical truths and strategies for parents who have adopted transracially will be explored in the following chapters.

## SUMMARY

Transracially adopting parents often find themselves intentionally clarifying appropriate (acceptable) and inappropriate (unacceptable) ways of interacting, including language, behavior, questions, and so on, for their extended family in light of the uniqueness of their adopted child. There are many things to consider.

1. Conversations within the family
   a. It's important to *start* the conversation. You don't have to know everything you'll even want to say about this important subject when you begin, but set a tone of open communication about this.
   b. Be sure to follow up on the conversation as life is shared, and acceptable and unacceptable instances occur.
2. Conversations within the context of your community
   a. What diversity do you find in your community (race, ethnicity, socioeconomic status, gender, sexual orientation, religion, and so on)?
   b. Are there key people within your community (neighbors, church leaders, teachers, principals, sports coaches, after-school program staff, and so on) whom you might need to approach with some of your ideas about appropriate and inappropriate language, behavior, and interactions?
   c. Are there other transracial families in your community? Consider finding allies among them.
3. Conversations with your child(ren)
   a. Be prepared to *start* the conversation. Take natural opportunities which arise in everyday life to enter this conversation over and over again.

## QUESTIONS

1. How comfortable are you as an adoptive parent in talking with your extended family directly about the implication of having a transracially adopted child in the family? What are your fears? What can motivate you to engage in this dialogue?
2. Are there allies, or people within your extended family, with whom you have had conversations about difference, prejudice, race, privilege, or bias? If so, whom? How might you build on those previous conversations to begin this new dialogue?
3. When inappropriate comments are made, unacceptable behavior is displayed, or undesirable events occur within the extended family in relation to your transracially adopted child(ren) or issues of race, how will you, as adoptive parents, respond? Work together to plan out possible responses. Who will take the lead with each family member if necessary?

4. Look for ways to approach these complex conversations from a place of curiosity, strength, opportunity, and beauty—not just caution—about what not to say and do.

## BIBLIOGRAPHY

Barber, B. (2012). Racial diversity increases, but segregation persists says geography professor. *Dartmouth Now*. Retrieved from http://now .dartmouth.edu/2012/06/racial-diversity-increases-but-segregation -persists-says-geography-professor/

Emerson, M. O., & Smith, C. (2000). *Divided by faith: Evangelical religion and the problem of race in America*. New York: Oxford University Press.

Grand, M. (2011). Excerpt. *Adoption Constellation*. http://adoptionconstellation .blogspot.com/p/excerpt.html

Payne, R. K., DeVol, P. E., & Dreussi Smith, T. (2006). *Bridges out of poverty: Strategies for professionals and communities*. Highlands, TX: aha! Process, Inc.

Quiroz, P. A. (2007). *Adoption in a color-blind society*. Lanham, MD: Rowman & Littlefield Publishers.

Schmitz, D. S. (2010). Developing an awareness of white privilege. *Reflections: Narratives of Professional Helping, 16*(1), 15–20.

# CHAPTER 4

# Hair as a Metaphor: Entering into the Culture of Your Child

## JANE HOYT-OLIVER AND JAYNE E. SCHOOLER

*It makes me worry about what my children have to deal with. It makes me sad . . . that people will sometimes just look at them on the outside and judge them and not see who they are on the inside.*

*Well, [transracial adoption] helped us to realize who our real friends are.*

*It takes a village to raise a child. (Ancient Nigerian proverb)*

*I just think that transracially adopting parents need to have the opportunity to be more educated because we're not educated, we're not. I spoke to the caseworkers at the agency and told them, you need to have a class right in the beginning for foster and adoptive parents called hair and skin care for African American children. That's the first cultural shock. It is something you have to deal with from day one. And white parents have not been taught it.*

## HAIR AS A METAPHOR: LOVING YOUR CHILD ENOUGH TO ASK FOR HELP FROM THOSE WHOM YOU MIGHT NOT KNOW

### CHALLENGES TO SEEKING HELP

All the adoptive parents in our study clearly loved their children deeply. There are a number of reasons why, when initially confronted with issues they did not know how to solve, the parents were reluctant to ask for help. These reasons are outlined below.

First, they may feel insecure in the role as adoptive parents. Parents want to be perceived as competent. They often want to demonstrate that they are good parents but mistakenly believe that a good parent will instinctually know what they child needs. So they fail to ask for help.

Second, they may not recognize that the community from which their children come may have solutions to their areas of concern. Families of color have information and life experience that Caucasian families do not. They are experts in the areas to be addressed later in this chapter, but families fail to ask.

A final possible reason is that parents believe that they should acculturate their children into a perceived "more successful" white culture. Because privilege has been or is the unspoken reality in the lives of many adopting parents, they expect that this acculturation will result in their children being granted the same privilege. By doing so, they invalidate the value and the uniqueness of their child's racial identity.

## RECOGNIZING AREAS OF NEED

In light of the discussion above, there are specific practical areas of need parents can address. One of the straightforward issues for which the families in our survey requested help from the community was the issue of grooming. African American children have skin and hair that need different care than the skin and hair of white children. Such issues surrounding grooming are both a concrete reality and a meta-phor for some of the difficult emotional terrain that transracially adopting parents must navigate, not only with their children but within the wider communities in which they live. Discussing these issues can provide strategies by which parents can become a part of their child's world, not simply expect the child to enter the parent's world.

When a child is adopted as an infant or at an early age, grooming is an issue that parents undertake. When they do, parents have choices as to how they will accomplish the task. As in many parent-ing experiences, these choices may be conscious, unconscious, or a combination of both, and may have both short term and long-term consequences.

Parents might

- Be unaware that the child's skin or hair might need different care than the skin and hair of the parent;
- Pretend that there is no difference in the grooming needs of the child;
- Know that there are difference in their child's grooming needs and ask for assistance from the members of the community to learn to care for the child's hair at home;
- Find a barbershop/hairdresser who can do a professional job when he or she might not be able to.

All of these responses have underling issues that affect the child, of course, but also may point to the parent's sense of his/her own self as a parent. With illustrations from a number of families, each response and the implications for the child and family will be discussed below.

### BEING UNAWARE THAT THE CHILD'S HAIR AND SKIN NEED DIFFERENT CARE

Most adoption agencies provide some information to adopting parents about the needs of the child, but some may not. In addition, the long term grooming needs of some children may not appear evident upon adoption. When Jim and Sandra adopted their two-month-old child, Steven, neither parent had much experience with children outside their own race. They were told their son, whose birth parents were of Asian, African, and European descent, might have dry skin as he grew older. They were shown his "Mongolian spot" and told to note that with their pediatrician, but did not remember any additional information about grooming given upon adoption. They lived in an overwhelmingly Caucasian community and had no additional reference points in terms of grooming or care. As the child grew, they openly admired his curly hair. The child would complain from time to time of an itchy scalp and would often have what they thought was dandruff. Utilizing knowledge from their own heritage, Jim and Sandra treated this condition with a variety of dandruff shampoos. They sought help from the child's barber (Jim and his son went together and had a fun "men's day out" once a month) but nothing seemed to make a difference. They even brought up the issue with the child's pediatrician, who prescribed a stronger hair product. It was not until their son was in college and with other mixed race children that he discovered that his hair, although "looking" like the curly hair of a Caucasian child, needed to be cared for with products and oils more suited to those used by his African American peers.

Jim and Sandra noticed a concern, and asked for help, but no one in their community was able to provide the information they needed to care for their son. As they look back, they realize the gaps in their own understanding, and have both talked this through and apologized to their now adult son.

## PRETENDING THAT THERE IS NO DIFFERENCE IN THE GROOMING NEEDS OF THE CHILD AND THE GROOMING NEEDS OF THE PARENT

Some parents may innately understand that their children have different grooming needs than the parents, but ignore those needs. These parents hope that by ignoring difference they may underscore the unity of their family, perhaps believing that by ignoring the need, they can also ignore that they are not biologically related to their child. This style of handling issues is much like the coping style within the general adoption experience—denial of differences (Schooler, 2006, p. 20). Because Franklin and his wife, Carolyn, had little or no understanding that their transracially adopted child would experience life differently from themselves, they never acknowledged those differences. Without a parent helping to navigate through those life experiences, a child is left to manage them on his own, which increases the sense of being different even within his own family.

## ASKING FOR ASSISTANCE FROM THE MEMBERS OF THE COMMUNITY TO LEARN TO CARE FOR THE CHILD'S HAIR

Many adults find that asking for help is difficult. They believe that asking for help underscores that they don't know how to best care for the child that they love. Parents who adopt may have the added concern that if they ask for help, others may also believe they don't know enough to care for their children—which may reinforce to the parent that s/he is not the birth parent and still has things to learn that might come as second nature to a parent who is identified as the same race as the child. This can increase anxiety about overall parenting skills or the fear that others will judge the adopting parent in the community.

Sometimes a chance encounter can provide parents with the help that they need. One of the moms in our study reached out to a stranger in a public place who was willing to extend help:

> *I was grocery shopping one day and I saw this woman. I said to my one year old, "Isn't her hair cool? I'd love to learn how to do that to your hair." She overheard me and said, "If you want me to show you how to do that, I will." I went over to her house one day and learned. And then I met another woman at the African American wellness walk and she came up to us and was talking about hair and she taught me how to do corn rows. So, I've learned if I get stumped, I usually have to ask somebody.*

The child's mom longed for help, but did not ask until help was offered to her by a stranger. From that chance encounter, this mom learned that asking for help can have a positive result for her child and for her own sense of being a good parent. This kind stranger provided the mom in the study with the opportunity to learn a new skill, which, in turn, provided her with a chance to care well for her daughter. These choices can both strengthen the parent-child bond and demonstrate a parent's respect for the needs of a child.

As with many learning experiences, parents may not get all the answers they need the first time they ask. In addition, they should not assume that *just because they ask*, people are going to be willing to help. One mom in our study was given incomplete advice about grooming on the day she first met her daughter as a foster child. She sought to find what she would need from her "traditional" sources, but then found she would need to go elsewhere. She contacted people who might be able to help, and those people connected her with others:

> *An African American foster mom at training told me to "just go and get some pink oil and throw it in her hair and you'll be fine." We went to my beauty shop first, but we ended up getting it at Wal-Mart. And I remember us using it on my daughter's hair; it was the most atrocious product. I thought there's got to be something that smells better than this. I called a friend of mine that I used to work with who was African-American and she wrote out a whole list of the right products to get and how I should start doing her hair. And I decided if we're going to do this, we're going to do it right.*

Three choices have been discussed regarding grooming care. There is one more.

## Finding a Barbershop/Hairdresser Who Can Do a Professional Job

Parenting is overwhelming. Parents are always getting accustomed to their new roles as parents; children are adjusting to the household. For some parents who know that their children will need hair cared for, the answer may be to take their child to a place where the child's needs can be met by those with professional experience: a barbershop or hair salon that specializes in the needs of the type of hair that the child might have. An additional bonus of such a choice, and an especially important one for those parents who live in predominantly Caucasian communities, is that they are provided with a predictable point in their monthly routine when they can interact with others who are identified as the same race as their child. This may require that parents go to a part of their community they rarely visit and where they do not "feel welcome," or, in some cases, go to a different community altogether. Some parents talk about being the "only person" of their race in the salon, and initially being treated as an outsider. Acknowledging that reality is important: equally important is the acknowledgement that your child may experience similar realities if she attends a school, worships, or participates in sports in a community where she is a racial minority. When discussing this issue, one parent in our study noted:

*All the nuances of daily life that are permeated with race, things that I wouldn't be able to even know about—some of them small, some of them not so small—I have to deal with because I'm a parent or that my kids have to be driven 45 minutes for my boys to get a haircut someplace. . . . you just see things differently.*

## Asking For and Receiving Help: If at First You Don't Succeed . . .

If one has not considered the idea of privilege in the past, or has not sustained direct contact with structural racism, parents may assume that if they ask for help, others will be willing to give it. This is not always the case. It may be that the parent will need to seek out several sources to gather the information needed to care for their child's skin and hair. Continue to do so. Doing so is very important. Keep searching. The search demonstrates that a parent doesn't know everything, but that the parent is willing to seek out anyone who can help with the identified needs. It builds a stronger bond between the parent and child based on the authentic needs of the child.

## STRATEGIES THAT USE THE COMMUNITY AS A RESOURCE FOR STRENGTHENING RESILIENCE

No parent can have all the answers all the time. Asking questions is how we learn to parent well. Finding people who have experience and who are willing to give helpful tips and perhaps sometimes honest criticism can be very important to successful parenting.

By the time many transracial children are formally adopted, they have had a number of adults act as their primary caregivers. Birth parents, relatives, and foster parents have had an impact on the children. Children have been exposed to a variety of worldviews, some of which may conflict with the parent's worldview. As adoption laws increasingly acknowledge the place of birth parents in the adoption process, and adoption practices increasingly provide space for birth parents and sometimes important extended birth family contact, the worldview of adopting parents will often be incorporated alongside the worldviews of the other important adults with whom the child has contact. One parent in our study had contact with the biological grandparents and a number of other biological relatives of her son. The relationship has been complex, because the biological family had very different worldviews, but after describing some of the complexities, the parent observed:

> The families are all different. They're all at different places in their lives. . . . It helps [our family] that the birth mother is not someone we've met, but we may. So that's another big worry. It's changed our lives. We've added friends.

Adopting parents should try to obtain as much information about other important adults in their child's life previous to the child's adoption so that when the child brings up issues and concerns, the adopting parents can address the child's issues within the context of the child's understanding. If parents ignore or downplay such issues when the child brings the issues up, then the parents are signaling that this issue is an area that *they* are uncomfortable talking about. If that occurs, their child may not feel he or she has "permission" to bring it up again. Even more of a concern is that the child may further feel that the issue is one that he or she will have to handle on his or her own.

## BE ATTUNED TO ISSUES THAT ARISE

Even though parents rarely used the words "white privilege" or "structural racism," participants in our study often recalled their child's own understanding of difference. These stories were often surprising and difficult for the parents; they found themselves, on the one hand, trying to reassure their child of his or her worth and value, while trying to figure out how much to say about the broader, structural issues. Caucasian parents are often astonished at how young their children are when these differences are brought up by the child, and wonder at what age it is appropriate to deepen the conversation about race and inequality. The best time, the authors believe, is when the child brings up the issue, no matter at what age the child wants to discuss her concerns. However, if the child does not bring issues of difference or race up, parents should find natural opportunities to do so when watching TV or movies, reading books with illustrations, or out in the community as a family. One parent recalled giving her three-year-old child a bath soon after the child was adopted; her daughter began washing herself and asked:

> "If I scrub hard enough will this color come off?" . . . I said, "Honey, do you know how much I would like to be the color that you are? You know, you have the most beautiful color." You know, because she truly is the most beautiful child you've ever seen. But she was determined that she was going to scrub that color off. So we had a lot of work to do right from the beginning.

## PAY ATTENTION TO THOSE WITHIN THE FAMILY'S CIRCLE OF INFLUENCE: THE POWER OF ROLE MODELS

Who the parents invite to their home as friends, who they speak of in admiring tones, and what issues are spoken of as important within the family will all have an impact on children. If parents do have friends of color and do ask for advice from those with more experience navigating the racialized world, children can be provided with strong role models and gain their own set of strategies to navigate successfully as they mature. Several couples in our study spoke about formal and informal groups that had helped them and their children:

*Another thing is in the school. I think there are two schools in [our area] that have this Parents of Black Children group. It was specifically named that way. And we have black parents and white parents. It was started by white parents in our school, a single mother who is not an adoptive mom. I've gotten involved with that.*

Some parents develop relational connections that meet the children's needs to see people of color in authority in their lives. In predominantly white communities, this may take a deliberate effort to enlist particular people to assist in routine para-parenting roles, then hoping that the selected persons can assist the parents and the children to gain insight into the nonwhite world. One parent noted:

*I've been trying to talk with people about how they prepare their children to deal with racism. . . . You know how; what do you say to your children? How do you teach them that just to find out what other families are doing? We have two girls who are in high school that babysit for us, and one is biracial and the other one is African American. And we look to them to be some support as somebody with whom our children can talk.*

Other adopting parents enlist the support of friends and other community members to provide support for their children. In a few cases, these relationships were already in place before the adoption took place, but in other cases the adopting parents worked to develop relationships with a group of people that might act as mentors to their children. Several examples are noted below:

*We had a couple of very good men friends who brought in some other friends who were acquaintances of ours who are now like our brothers, we're all just a very tight group of people. A couple of African American men, it's a mixed group. Some gays, some straight, men of color, white men, varying levels of education and work histories, and professional pursuits. . . . and we got together once a week and took our son out for dinner and would do "manly things" we would say. So, he still spends one afternoon on the weekend and one evening a week with the men. . . . yeah, that's really incredible. One of the guys, you know, lives with us part time, and, you know, it's really an interesting mix. You know, we're talking about getting a house with another one of the guys and getting a triple-decker. Because we are each other's family.*

*We are exposed to quite a number of very successful black families who just really have it going on; they have strong parents, good kids, the parents expect a lot of the kids, the kids are successful and happy and proud . . . and so the kids see that they have that role model.*

*We developed an adoptive support group. Another family who has adopted, we just felt they were really a strong family. They're a black family and they adopted a black child. They have two biological children also. We met them through an adoption picnic. And they're like Aunt S. and Uncle J. That's how they're referred to in our family. And so, we see them all the time. We also are friends with three adult women in this neighborhood who had been transracially adopted as children and I probably wouldn't have met any of them had I not had these children.*

## SEEK ADVICE FROM THOSE OF THEIR CHILD'S RACE

The parents in our study were very concerned about the impact of racism on their children. All parents in our study had spoken to their children about race and prejudice. When asked whether it was a high priority to encourage their children to seek support and advice from adults of his or her race about coping with prejudice, 74 percent either strongly or moderately agreed. Many parents indicated they had to teach children coping strategies to deal with racially-based teasing, although these strategies were quite wide ranging: from addressing the issue head on by addressing it with their parents or other authority figures, to telling their children that "not everyone will like you, so it is best to let it go." All indicated that they had "identified parental responsibilities related to race and culture." Parents also indicated a strong desire to help their children establish relationships with adults of the child's birth culture, with over 70 percent indicating their either "strongly "or "moderately" agreed with this statement. One mom remarked:

*Privilege as a concept was a theoretical concept to me and one that I could relate to in terms of some forms of discrimination that I experienced as a Jew. But the reality of it I think didn't hit me until we had our son.*

Later in the interview, she noted:

*I don't know that we have strategies, so much as just talking about the issues. You know, so, never skirting the issue of what it means to be black in this society.*

This mother observed that the marginalization her son experienced because of his race was more difficult than what she had experienced as a member of a less powerful religious group. She speaks eloquently to the deeply entrenched reality of a racialized country.

Parents in our study also found that as they grew as a family and viewed the world not only through a lens of white privilege but through the experiences of their children, they became sensitive to the racialized world. One dad noted:

*You have to be very intentional about your life. Before [we adopted], we didn't have to think about anything like where will we go to church, where would we live, where [would our children] go to school, where will there be other people that look like us. . . . I think you have the luxury of not thinking about that when you're not a mixed family; [with a mixed family] you have to be very aware or you get aware in a hurry.*

*I would say our neighbors, our immediate neighbors, when we first adopted were very supportive. And we've only had really negative experience from Christian folks who were very old school thinking. . . . I think I'm more aware when I walk into a room of whether it's a diverse group or not. It's instantaneous for me now, whereas I think a lot of people are oblivious. . . . And then not just with African Americans, but just diverse groups in general.*

## THE CHALLENGES OF ADVOCATING FOR YOUR CHILD

Every loving parent has concerns for their children. Parents want to create the optimal balance between protection for their children and providing each one with the skills by which the child can succeed in life. A good deal of the toolkit that each parent brings to that task is initially learned from his or her family of origin: these ideas and skills form the "default position" that parents bring to the early years of parenting. Of course, as they live together, parents adapt to the child and the child adapts as well: this happens as personalities intersect, as the family shares experiences both wonderful and tragic, and, of course, as the child matures and comes into contact with societal institutions such as the school, places of worship, and other community institutions. But a number of studies indicate that the impact of racialization complicates these issues. Emerson and Smith wrote that Caucasian families often assume that the choices that parents and children make overwhelmingly determine either a positive or a negative outcome; for example, if a child has talent, and works to develop that talent, society will recognize both the talent and effort and reward the child with good grades and recognition (Emerson & Smith, 2000). This perception, which holds well enough for white middle class and upper class families, is not always the case for children of color.

A number of parents in our study were surprised to discover this reality. They were dismayed and perplexed by the reaction of others when they attempted to intervene on behalf of their children in school or at church because they believed their child had been neglected or wronged. They often found that the leaders within the institution downplayed and in some cases refused to listen to the parent's concerns, negating the observations/information provided by parents. Most Caucasian parents expect to be taken seriously and have been anticipating a certain amount of respect from authorities in such institutions, but instead find when they bring concerns to authorities about racism or issues of concern for their children's treatment, they are met with denial or indifference. Several examples are noted below:

*The darker kids were placed in the [special needs] program. When we walked into the special ed. classroom, we did a double-take. We were the only white folks in there. Everything that we did to try to advocate on his behalf just made it worse.*

*I remember I picked up our oldest one day and he had detention in junior high. And I said, "What did you do that required detention]?" And he said, "Passing notes." And I said, "And why were you passing notes?" And he said, "Well, this girl called me a name and I passed a note back to her that wasn't very kind and they found mine, but not hers." And I*

*said, "And what name did she call you?" And he said, "Oh, Mom, that's
a given." And, of course, I knew he meant nigger.*

*We went and talked to the principal beforehand and shared all kinds
of stuff. And the principal thought and said, "We don't have any Hispanic kids, and we don't have any kids with two moms in the school, or
kids with gay and lesbian parents." And I thought, "I know you do
because I know who they are." It really troubles me that they aren't
known to you. That says something.*

Caucasian parents in such situations may need to find additional
sets of cultural tools to protect and nurture their children. It is in such
situations that ongoing connections with adults who have struggled
with similar injustices can provide insight as well as recommend strategies that will strengthen a child's self-concept. Parents who adopt
transracially must make a concerted effort to understand the world
from the perspective of the African American community both for
their children's sake and for their own.

African American families hold information about how to live
within the United States *as people of color* that the vast majority of
Caucasians do not have. This information may be important for
appearances' sake, such as where might a young woman of color buy
makeup that matches her skin tone, since much of the makeup mar-
keted even in "high-end" department stores in her neighborhood
do not compliment darker skin tones. Or the information may be
literally life-saving, such as, if one's son is a young black male, how
to act if one is stopped by the police, or how one reacts when one
lives in a state that allows armed citizens to "stand your ground." As
readers will note, some information is quite straightforward and
some far more subtle. Parents need to seek out parents of color, to
ask questions (with humility: taking the position that they do not
know what they need to know), and to listen well to the answers that
are offered.

## SHOULD WE FIT IN OR CELEBRATE
## OUR DIFFERENCE?

One way several of the parents dealt with these realities was to elect
to "join" their children in marginalization. These parents had recognized that not just their children, but the family unit itself was often
viewed as being "different." They decided essentially that family unity

is preferable to conformity. The dad who spoke of needing to be deliberate about where his family lived and where they worship remarked:

> *I feel my children's sense of alienation. I feel their outsiderness. I put*
> *myself in their place of being an outsider. And that's the painful thing.*
> *And not only in the family, but everywhere. So you kind of join hands*
> *with them and stand on the outside and then you're all on the outside*
> *together.*

Although the research focused on transracially adopting parents,
attitudes don't occur in a vacuum. Parents are affected by their children's sense of self. And, like children everywhere, transracially
adopted children may struggle with their own identity as they mature
no matter how much parents desire to protect them from such struggles. Some parents find that as their children mature and begin to
embrace their own sense of racial identity, the cultural dissonance of
living with parents of a different race may cause the child to emotionally or even physically withdraw from the parents. One parent described
this particularly painful situation with his two teen-aged children:

> *Both of them are operating within a universe with things that don't*
> *quite fit. And they're struggling with it all the time. Like little stuff,*
> *like when we drop them off at school or something, you know they want*
> *to be dropped off around the corner because they don't want to be seen*
> *being dropped off by a white parent.*

## HAIR AS A METAPHOR: STRENGTHENING YOUR FAMILY THROUGH CONNECTION WITH OTHERS

So, how can parents assist their children to thrive in a racialized
society? First and foremost, parents should honestly acknowledge the
things that they can give to their children and what they cannot bring.
Parents have many gifts they can give to their children. Although each
set of parents brings a different mix of gifts, these often include critical assets such as security, stability, love, compassion, honesty, and
faith. But the very best parents also acknowledge that they cannot
bring everything that their child may need to develop to the child's
full potential. Just as a parent with little musical ability might hire a
teacher or seek out a talented neighbor if her child wants to learn how
to play a musical instrument, parents need to seek out members of the

child's racial or ethnic community for their assistance with issues that the parents do not know how to address. As many of the couples in our study have done, reaching out means acknowledging the parent "doesn't have all the answers," but paradoxically, by asking questions and listening well, parents have far *more* answers than they would have had without asking. Parents who ask for help are often better parents, because they are willing to look for answers to what they don't know.

In addition to this very basic work of connecting with others, parents should immerse themselves in the movies, literature, and history of the child's culture. Even well into the second decade of the 21st century, the authors deplore the lack of in depth information provided to students about the contributions of people of color in the basic history courses within most high schools. However, there are wonderful films, books, and music that can detail the amazing accomplishments of those whom history has overlooked. This immersion can have the great benefit of providing the parents with a better understanding of how the community as a whole has contributed to the larger story of this country. One of the authors recalls going to the movie theater to see *The Original Kings of Comedy* (2000) with her husband. Although the theater was almost full there were very few (she counted fewer than 20) other Caucasian people in the theater. Often we think that humor is universal, but despite its veneer of universality, even comedy has its racial fault lines. Learning about and celebrating the wide spectrum of contributions that have been made by people of color can strengthen a parent's ability to care for and empower their children.

If children observe those they love and trust easily speaking about such contributions, this can become a powerful and corrective testimony that can strengthen a child's own sense of place within history. In addition, such interest by the parent shows the child that the parent finds this history important. Finally, the parent's increased knowledge can assist the child to take on some of that learning, providing fodder for family discussions that may never have taken place around the dinner tables when the parents were themselves children.

One note about this remedial work: be prepared to also deal with painful realities. For example, when one of the authors of this book did research about slavery in New England before the Civil War, she discovered that members of her family had owned slaves, and that the son of one of the slaves had been sent South to a relative so he would remain in bondage when the state had "emancipated" the children of those who were in bondage. Learning this was deeply painful;

discussing this reality with her daughter of color (who was, at the time a young adolescent) was also painful. The parents in this situation opted to be honest with their daughter, which in turn reinforced that her parents would be honest with her even when things were tough. This, in turn, reinforced that the foundation of this family was honesty and a willingness to deal together with what is "real" in their family's life.

In summation, parents do not know everything that they will need to know about their children or about what each child will need before the child is placed in the parents' home. The main job of a parent *isn't* to know everything, but to know when to ask for help, to have people to whom you can turn when help is needed, and if there are no people whom one knows who might help, to seek out help from those who might be willing to act as a "community connector" and answer questions. This might even mean going back to the agency that facilitated the adoption and asking caseworkers for assistance or for referrals. Finding the courage to ask will not only lead to a way for getting answers, it will demonstrate to your child the length to which you are willing to go to get the help he or she needs to become a strong and resilient adult. No one can do it all; it truly does take a village to raise a child well.

## SUMMARY

One of the most critical and ongoing responsibilities for transracially adoptive parents is to recognize racial stereotypical experiences for their children, and to develop keen awareness and attunement to their child's emotion experiences and needs. How can this be done?

1. Expand ones' understanding of history and race in relation to your child's race.
2. Learn about the skin and hair needs of their transracially adopted children. It will be different than the parents'.
3. Recognize there is a difference in grooming needs, realizing that not doing so can impact the child's self-esteem and even identity.
4. Be proactive in asking for help from those within the community.
5. Understand the challenges involved in advocating for your child in school and within the community and become a pro-active advocate, not waiting until a crisis demands it.

## QUESTIONS

1. When is the last time you had a conversation with your child about his life experiences outside the home?
2. From whom do you seek help and advice regarding the grooming needs of your child?
3. In what ways have you found it difficult to find the help you need for the holistic needs of your child?
4. What experiences/encounters can you relate to that were discussed in this chapter?
5. How did you handle those experience/encounters? Would you do anything differently?

## BIBLIOGRAPHY

Emerson, M. O., & Smith, C. (2000). *Divided by faith: Evangelical religion and the problem of race in America.* New York: Oxford University Press.

Schooler, J. (2006). *The whole life adoption book.* Colorado Springs, CO: Pinon Press.

# CHAPTER 5

# In His Voice: Kevin

## KEVIN HOFMANN

## BEGINNINGS

As I took my first breath in the summer of 1967 in Central Park West Hospital in Detroit, Michigan, the city was still smoking from the riots that began two and a half weeks before. One early Sunday morning the blacks collectively stood up and spoke out against the oppression they felt from the predominately white police force. On that morning, at an after-hours club where a group of friends and relatives gathered to welcome home two black Vietnam vets, the Detroit police greeted the party goers and began hauling out the celebrants and taking them downtown. As the police realized they had grossly underestimated the size of the party, they had to wait for backup to arrive. Meanwhile, the nearby homeowners joined the scene and the crowd began to grow. It was at this moment the blacks in the city decided to stand up against the routine discriminatory practices acted out towards blacks.

The tension between the races had been building and building to this point, and as the tension rose I was born. I am the product of an affair between my white mother and black father who worked together in the Chevrolet Stamping Plant in Detroit. As the city was splitting along racial lines my parents came together to create me. I was immediately placed for adoption as my parents retreated to their homes and back to their spouses and families.

After three months in foster care, I was placed with a white minister, his wife, and their three biological children in their home in Dearborn, Michigan, a happy-to-be-white suburb of Detroit. The community and the Lutheran church where my father was an assistant pastor openly protested my presence in the community. The protest culminated in a cross being burned in our front yard when I was only ten months old. After living three years in a community that didn't want us, my parents moved the family to Detroit where my father pastored a segregated church where the parsonage was located in a black community. After living and playing with children that looked like me from age three to eight my father was promoted and we moved again, just two miles away from the black neighborhood. We were still in Detroit but now lived in a white community where I was the only child of color.

I felt fortunate because I still maintained contact with children of color in the schools that I attended. From kindergarten to twelfth grade I went to schools where the student body was about 95 percent black. After that, I would leave the comfort of Detroit and those that looked like me to attend Alma College in Alma, Michigan, a small private college in the middle of corn fields. The colors of my life would change again and the culture shock that came with it made my head spin.

I have lived a colorful life as a transracial adoptee and through these wonderfully difficult changes in environment, I have learned much. It is my pleasure to share from the life I have lived to help those children who come behind me. There is a purpose to my life, and it is to help smooth out the paths walked by other transracial adoptees and their families.

I currently live in Toledo, Ohio, with my wife (I married a black woman . . . everyone always wants to know but is afraid to ask) and two teenage boys. Now that I am a father of two black boys, I have a clear view of how society views young men of color and, sadly, although we have a person of color in the White House, the ugliness that my children face is much worse than the racism I grew up with. Because of this, the lessons I have learned are still very relevant today, even more so than when I grew up. It is often assumed that we live in a postracial society and part of my job is to share the harsh truth so today's multicultural families are aware and can adjust and/or fine tune their approach to living as a multicultural family.

I have often told those I meet "I'm a minority in my own family. I was found in the wilderness and I was raised by a pack of wild Caucasians."

Being a transracial adoptee (TRA) was a great way to start a conversation—especially during my teenage dating years. Nothing broke the ice easier than telling of my unusual family. While I was surrounded by our colorful family, I'm not sure I understood the gravity and breadth of what it meant to be part of a transracial family. Besides supplying an unusual pick-up line, what did it mean to me to be transracially adopted?

As an adult adoptee I think about this a lot and reflect upon the impact of being from a multicultural family and how that has shaped my life. In thinking about my life as a TRA, I often flash back to a simple conversation I heard over and over.

*"So, he's your* brother?*" the confused kids would say to my brother when the adults were no longer around.*

*"Yep," my brother would say. He was very rehearsed for the conversation.*

*"How is he your brother? He's black!" the confused kids would say, trying to solve this genetic mystery.*

*"He's adopted," my brother would respond.*

*"What happened to his* real *mom?" the confused kids would ask.*

*"She couldn't take care of him, so she put him up for adoption," my brother would say in his "this is just how it is" voice.*

The kids would accept this answer initially and the conversation would dissolve into the next subject or the next game of tag.

This conversation happened around me quite a few times. It was a conversation my siblings had a lot and I overheard it more when in the presence of our parents. Those answers my brother gave were answers he heard our parents say to confused adults and after a while they just became the answers. As I said, this conversation often happened within my earshot as if I wasn't there. This small conversation sent a lot of interesting messages to me as a young child growing up. To be discussed as if you are not in the room can make you feel pretty insignificant. As an adoptee, I come predisposed to feeling insignificant because no matter how you cut it, my mother gave me away. When coupled with this conversation *and* the way society made me feel like a second class citizen as a child of color, it created an insurmountable self-esteem mountain.

This conversation labeled me as *adopted*. My family said, "He's adopted" in the present tense. Therefore, being adopted became part of me whether I liked it or not. Fortunately, there were many things I enjoyed about being adopted. But often being introduced to people in this manner made it difficult to separate myself from this legal description that fails to describe who I am.

The questions about my "real" mother were confusing because the failsafe answer, "She couldn't take care of him . . ." doesn't make any sense to me even today. I had many friends whose parents had neither the financial ability or the emotional ability to care for them, but they didn't give them away. This answer never told me the real reason why, so I deduced that there was something broken in me which caused my mother to give me away. The self-esteem mountain got steeper and steeper.

The messages that are conveyed by not saying something can often be more powerful than what is spoken. The conversation above is a good example of what was and wasn't said and the messages I drew from that. Very often I get asked about the secret formula—what it takes to raise confident, happy, well-adjusted transracial adoptees— and the answer I continue to come back to is simple at first blush. Being a parent in a transracial family is a very, very purposeful job. It means understanding the potential struggles your child may have and proactively addressing them. It means purposefully sending very clear messages that will build up your child and guard against the unspoken messages. So it is with design and purpose that parents must fashion their multicultural lives. It means addressing, talking about, reading about, researching, and studying the impact of the 3 C's: Commitment, Color, and Culture.

## COMMITMENT

When I was three years old our family packed up the contents of our large suburban home set in the quiet white community of Dearborn, Michigan, and moved six miles east to a black neighborhood in Detroit. Dearborn was a very happy-to-be-white community and my splash of color unnerved many people. So my parents made a life-changing decision for our family. They chose to move into a black neighborhood where I would be surrounded by children and adults that shared my skin tone. It was in that neighborhood that the seeds of my racial identity were planted.

Initially, when my parents made the decision to adopt me they assumed that simply giving me a loving home would cure all that may have ailed me and society. Fortunately for me, our neighbors and fellow church members let it be known right away that love would never erase the color of my skin. I say fortunately because it was with this realization that my parents had to decide where would be the best place to live as a multicultural family. If the community hadn't been so vocal we may have stayed in that community and the quiet messages whispered by a fellow classmate about what my skin color meant to them would have changed me. Growing up as one of the only children of color in a majority environment is a heavy burden for a young child to balance and juggle. So the intolerant environment in Dearborn forced my parents to make a decision that would positively impact my quality of life at age three.

As a multicultural family, decisions like this one have to be purposeful, focused, and for the greater good. My parents were committed to the multicultural family they created. They pulled their chairs in and pushed their chips to the center of the table; they were all-in. Included in those chips was their all-access pass to white privilege. They would still retain the basic benefits of white privilege but the deluxe membership was given away and they were alright with their decision. It would mean often they would be a minority, it would mean often they were seen as outsiders, and it would mean getting to see life as their child of color would someday see life. This decision and resulting experience meant later in life, when I was struggling with being a minority in this world, my parents understood what that meant, what it felt like, what it smelled and tasted like, and could support me from a genuine place.

I hear you.

There are some who will read this and say, "We don't have the means to move." To which I respond, so what is your level of commitment? What are you willing to do to place your child in an environment where they are in contact with people who look like them?

Back in 1967 when I was adopted I was considered a hard-to-place, special needs adoption. In some areas today children of color are still considered hard-to-place, special needs adoptions, and I agree with that classification. Children of color have special needs that must be met. Many will balk at the thought of moving to place their child closer to a community of color, but if they had a special needs child who required special therapy that was 45 minutes away four times a week, they would do it and may even consider moving closer to the therapist. Many have told me they can't or won't move—and I don't think everyone needs to—but will you be willing to put your child in a sports league across town in a different neighborhood to get them the connections as well as the training they need? It means committing to doing something purposeful that will improve your child's quality of life.

## COLOR

When we moved to the black neighborhood, the children I played with showed me what black was and I was sold. I wanted to be like them, modeled the way I talked and walked to be more like them, and they showed me the many wonderful hues that come with being a child of color. It is because of those children that I never once wished I was anything but black. It was because of my contact with children that looked like me that I accepted myself as a child of color. I remember during those adolescent years feeling sorry for my white brothers and sister because they didn't have the opportunity to be one of the cool kids like me.

I grew up in the '70s, when there was very little positive representation of blacks in the media. My role models on TV were characters like Fred Sanford from *Sanford and Son*, a very poor wisecracking black male, or the Evans family from *Good Times*, a very poor wisecracking family. There was no depth to these characters. They were more stereotypes than role models. I was glad I had access to the real thing. I saw in my black friends superheroes. The way they walked through life inspired me and from them I gained invaluable tools that helped sustain me later in life.

My best friend was bulletproof. He was about five years older than me and nothing affected him. You couldn't say anything that would crack his tough exterior. He walked like he owned the moon. I was his understudy and would often try on his bravado. It was always too big but eventually I grew into it.

After living in the black neighborhood for five years, our family moved two miles away to a white neighborhood still in Detroit. I was still going to schools that were about 95 percent black, so my contact with children of color continued. When I first went out to play in the new neighborhood, I wore the armor that was passed down to me by those black kids in the previous neighborhood. That armor protected me in an environment that was initially hostile. I was the different one and it was pointed out all the time.

For the first time in my life, I was powerless. I was outnumbered and the thoughts and feelings of the majority and what their parents were telling them were being shot at me. Most of it was done out of ignorance, and some was done to see how the new black kid would react when he was tested. The armor deflected the insults that were hurled at me. On the outside it appeared I was unshaken. When the weapons were thrown in my direction, there was no explosion, there was no effect, and so the weapons were recalculated and thrown at someone else who appeared armorless. In my quiet moments when I was able to take off my armor, my wounds were very real. They hurt and they took time to heal. But they healed much quicker when they weren't being reopened again and again.

Now I know this is a very powerful coping mechanism many people of color use subconsciously to deal with racism. It often displays itself in the form of a very loud, tough, obnoxious personality designed to keep people at a distance where they are unable to hurt you. It was one of the most valuable tools I have ever been given and it was a tool that my parents never could have given me because they weren't aware of its existence.

We never talked about race in our house when we were growing up. It wasn't that my parents didn't want to talk about it. I just think they didn't know how to start the conversation and after a while it just became part of our family culture to not talk about it. I think part of the reason was that my parents were waiting for me to bring it up and when I never did they assumed it wasn't important to me. I was fortunate in that I had my black friends whom I could talk to about how race and racism were affecting me. The assumption often is that adoptees will bring things up when they want to talk about them. Looking back on it now, that is not a job I should have been saddled with as a child. It is the parents' responsibility to commit to talk about the tough things, including race, racism, prejudice, and adoption as well.

In the presence of those that shared like experiences was my place to exhale. I remember often going to my black friends and simply saying something like, "I think Mrs. Matz down the street doesn't like me because I'm black."

My friends knew what that was like and understood it was possible and their response was calming. They would just say something like, "Man, that is messed up." I didn't need them to try and justify it away or argue that I was interpreting things wrong. I just needed someone to hear me. This simple response let me know it may not be me but rather her inadequacies. That meant a lot.


## TALKING ABOUT RACE

So how does a parent talk about race?

I have two teenage black sons and we talk about race all the time. My wife and I understood it was important for them to understand how the world perceives race and more importantly how the world perceives them as black boys.

The easiest way to talk about race is to talk about race. The media is constantly talking about it, so join in on the conversation. I remember when it made the news that a black Harvard professor was arrested on his own front porch. He had just returned home from vacation and a neighbor saw him trying to get in to his own front door. The neighbor assumed the black man was an intruder instead of a neighbor. The police were called and the professor and the police got into an argument on his front porch and he was arrested. I remember sitting in the living room when this story was on the TV and I simply turned to my sons and explained to them what happened, what the police did wrong, what the professor did wrong, and what to do if they are ever in a similar situation. This was an easy way to talk about a tough subject while at the same time it wasn't personal. It was easier talking about what someone else did and could have done better while making it a teaching moment. My kids were both adolescents when we had that conversation. This wasn't the first time we talked with them about race either. We always talked about race. We never avoided it, assuming if we don't talk about it they won't be affected by it. We, as parents, understood the reality that they would be affected by race, so we needed them to understand what will be going on around them and to them.

As transracial parents, it is your job to balance the scales for your child. There are so many messages that get sent to children of color about their skin. The Clark Doll Test demonstrated that very clearly in the '50s, and even when done today brings the same results. Children learn early on darker skin color equals bad. So you as a transracial parent have to balance the messages that children are getting on a daily basis and you can't do that if you ignore the conversation of race and ignore that their skin color is different. You have to rewrite the definitions and show them different isn't bad.

## CULTURE

Being exposed to other black children was a wonderful educational process for me. Being in contact with kids who were raised in black households gave me hands on experience of black culture. It was from these children I learned what was acceptable and what wasn't in the black community and I became a student of the culture.

As a transracial adoptee a lot of my energy was put in to just blend-ing into the black community. So I sat back and just observed and learned how to blend. My biggest fear was being seen as a fraud by those in the black community. Just as any other child, I just wanted to be a part of the group.

A few years ago I went to my 30th reunion for my grade school. I sat talking to a friend I hadn't seen in decades and when she asked me what I was doing, I told her about the book I wrote about my experi-ence as a transracial adoptee. The woman I was speaking to stopped me in mid-sentence and said, "I didn't know you were adopted!" When she said that the Hallelujah chorus went off in my head: what I worked so hard at, what I put so much energy into had worked. She simply just saw me as another black peer and I was relieved. At 44 years old, I was relieved.

What came so easily to my black peers was something I had to study and practice and learn. It was the cultural cues that I had to adopt that helped me to just blend in. Each cultural group has its own rules, customs, beliefs, and traditions. If you don't understand them and know how to act or react to certain things at certain times, you will easily be found out. If you don't blend in and pick up on those hidden cultural rules, you stand the chance of being labeled an outsider and membership into that community will be revoked.

When I was in college, I pledged a fraternity for two weeks. The college I went to was largely white and again just wanting to fit in, I thought if I could align myself with a group, maybe they would forget I was black. During rush week the fraternities were nice, interested, and anxious to get to know me. Well, all but one fraternity. One fra-ternity on the campus of the small liberal arts college had the reputa-tion of being very anti-non-white. Their reputation rang true for me and they showed no interest in recruiting me and it was obvious my skin color was the reason for it. I was pledging during the fall semester and soon after I made my decision to pledge the fraternity that I saw as the most liberal and diverse. Homecoming weekend was upon us. This meant that many alumni would be returning to campus and those who were revered as godlike in the fraternity would return to test the new pledges. One of the simplest tests was in the greeting. Once introduced to the alumni, we would shake hands. It was my job to remember to initiate the fraternity's secret handshake. It was within that split second the alumni would make a decision. If I did the hand-shake right I was welcomed into their secret circle. I had passed the first test. The next tests would come in a series of quizzes. The alumni would quiz me about fraternity history. If I was up on my history, the vetting would continue. It was a very stressful weekend and my first impressions were mixed. There were some members who thought I had earned the right to be a part of the fraternity. There were others who thought I was not worthy and they shunned me immediately. They didn't feel I was worthy to be a part of their culture, their secret society. A few weeks later I quit. The hazing and constant evaluation of me became too much. The armor that I was given by my black peers early in life told me to move on. The constant tight rope walk of trying to do the right thing to be accepted was exhausting. So I reached deep into my closet, pulled out my armor, and walked away. I did it with the exterior bravado of a prizefighter, but inside I was heartbroken to be rejected again.

Looking back on this experience now, I realize this was stuffed full of issues, lessons, reminders, and flashbacks of many things that I am very sensitive to as an adoptee. The desire to fit in and not be rejected was strong and a large reason why this was such a painful experience for me. The work that went in to trying to fit into this new culture, trying to remember the cultural cues, the cultural history, beliefs, traditions, and so on reminds me of what it was like growing up. Constantly being on guard, trying to remember the correct response in different situations, sucked the energy out of me. My 21-year-old mind was taxed enough with trying to get through college. I understood a lot of my classmates would believe the stereotypes that blacks were inferior so I put a lot of my energy into proving them wrong, which meant I had to study like I never had before. The prize of being part of the fraternity wasn't worth it. Being accepted into that culture wasn't the same as the black culture so the investment wasn't worth my time and energy. Being accepted into the black culture was the ultimate prize for me growing up. I understood early on in life that if I wasn't accepted in to the black community, there was no alternative. I knew the white community would not accept me as part of their community. So the studying, the learning, the practicing was worth the end-game.

There were times when the rules of the black community were hard lessons to learn. When I was in high school I often would go over to my friend Tyrone's house. I would go to the side door of Tyrone's home and knock to pick him up to go out and do something that usually involved young ladies. Tyrone would meet me at the door and we would walk up the three small steps in to the kitchen where his mother always was standing at the stove cooking. It didn't matter what day or what time of day it was, she was *always* standing at the stove cooking and the smells and vapors that arose from the skillet she cooked in were unlike anything I ever experienced before. She cooked things I never had at my house. This was one of the things that I mourned as a transracial adoptee. Food is such a big part of black culture and I was unaware and out of touch with this piece of black culture. This is one of the gaps that comes with being a transracial adoptee. There are pieces of culture you may be aware of but lack the intimate knowledge that most children have that grow up in that culture. So, although I grew up connected to black culture, I still had deficiencies in several areas, and food and black music were my Achilles heel. Whenever these subjects came up with my black peers I would cringe because I lacked the knowledge base to speak on them. It was times like these that I dreaded because I was sure someone would point out my lack of "blackness."

Tyrone's mother stood at the stove stirring in the skillet with her back to me every time I entered their home. His mother was mean and very strict and I sensed she didn't like me, so I made sure to avoid all contact with her. She scared me and I was uncomfortable around her, which is why I did what I did. I ascended the three steps up in to the kitchen and hoped to just sneak past her on the way to Tyrone's room so he could finish getting ready before we left. I never said a word to her and broke a cultural rule I was unaware existed.

The next day Tyrone stopped me at school and told me that if I wanted to continue hanging out with him, his mother said I better not ever come into her house and not speak to her. The level of disrespect that I showed her in her mind was unmeasurable, but she was willing to give me one more chance. From that day on I always spoke as soon as I entered their home and when I exited. It was a rule that has been branded on my brain.

A few years ago, I was speaking in Detroit and I invited Tyrone to come. After I was done I introduced Tyrone to the crowd of transracial parents who had come to hear me share from my experience. Instantly, one of the transracial mothers in the group turned to Tyrone and asked what it was like growing up with a friend who was raised by white parents. Tyrone then shared with us a belief that is often held in the black community about white families that his mother applied to my family. Tyrone explained that the reason why his mother didn't like me was because I was raised by a white family and her belief was that white families often lack the discipline needed to raise respectful children. Unfortunately, my actions in her aroma-filled kitchen only cemented her beliefs. Tyrone went on to say that any time he was disrespectful to his mother, she would say, "See, you are picking up bad habits from that Kevin boy."

I was oblivious to this growing up. I was aware she didn't like me but I assumed, as I often did when I was slighted, that there was something about me that was damaged or broken and that is why she didn't like me.

The beliefs and ideas around respect and the role that older people play in the black community was an example of some of the cultural rules and beliefs I didn't know or understand and often those rules and beliefs were learned the hard way. But it was through my connection with the black community that I learned them. I cherish the passing down of the knowledge today no matter how it was learned. I cherish it because through that connection and through that knowledge I have options.

Many people look at transracial adoptees and wonder who we will grow up to be more comfortable around. They wonder if we will be more comfortable around people that reflect our family or people who reflect our skin tone. Today, I am much more comfortable around people who share my same skin tone because we share like experiences. Other people of color understand the daily slights and prejudices I face and being able to share that with someone else who understands that is my place to exhale. But . . . if I hadn't been exposed to that culture early on in life, I would not know how to move in that environment and my inability to move in that environment would mean I would be rejected from that environment; being exposed to black culture created options for me. I now have options as to which environment I can move in and I actually feel comfortable in both to a certain degree. I understand the power of race so when in a majority white environment I look at things through a lens that allows me to recognize the smallest slight. This has come from over 40 years of living as a person of color and has nothing to do with paranoia. When in a predominately black environment I am allowed to unstrap the armor and exhale. I don't need to analyze words and actions and I can just relax. I wouldn't have this oasis if I hadn't learned the rules and been exposed to them, but because I was, I have the option and ability to move in the black community comfortably.

## INSIGHTS FOR PARENTS

It has been through these 3 Cs, Commitment, Color, and Culture, that my life has been enhanced. I enjoy and enjoyed growing up as a transracial adoptee. The uniqueness that comes with being a minority in my own home has always fed my need for attention as an adoptee. I stand out because of this uniqueness and that's alright with me. The importance of transracial parents committing to their multicultural family's needs is paramount. All cultures in the family should be celebrated and recognized as an integral part of the family's makeup.

Recognizing color and the way society views it is also paramount. Walking through life blind to color is not a realistic way to experience life. Children see color, we all see color, and children look to their parents to define what that difference means. Ignore the difference and you send the opposite message than you are intending to send. Instead of the message of inclusion, the absence of color conversations sends the message of inferiority and exclusion.

Culture and putting your children in connection with their culture is also important. The understanding that you can't teach your children what you don't know is invaluable. You must be willing to find a cultural surrogate that will help teach your children the hidden rules and beliefs of their culture. If your children learn the culture, then they will be awarded access to a rich and powerful culture that whispers to them that they are more powerful. These whispers help silence the shouts that come from a society that tells them they are less.

# CHAPTER 6

# Parenting between Cultures: Important Considerations for Parents

## JANE HOYT-OLIVER

Previous chapters have described some of the important issues that are faced by couples when they choose to become transracially adopting parents. This chapter will provide information to assist parents as they parent their children. The chapter focuses on three important aspects of parenting: identity development, formation of self-esteem, and power. It is the authors' intention that by sharing this information, families will increase their ability to think through issues of race and racism as they arise and place those issues in the context of their children's development and growth.

### IDENTITY DEVELOPMENT

Researchers Emily Upshur and Jack Demick noted that a person's identity is central to his or her well-being (2006). They define *identity* as an "integrated, coherent, and goal-directed self . . . which is critical to well-being and psychological adjustment" (p. 92). Individuals develop an identity by assessing who they are in the context of the community. For example, they listen to what is said by the people who are important to them (e.g., family, friends, and others), but also by those who do not know them well, or may not know them at all. In chapter five, Kevin Hofmann suggested parents could read books and magazines and watch television to discover how the people with whom their children might identify are portrayed in the media. If they have people they can talk to about these issues, they can check their own perceptions with those they consider trustworthy and/or important. This process, called *identity formation* or *identity development*, is one human beings engage in during their lifetime. Although researchers now believe human beings form identity throughout life, the process is often most openly observable during adolescence and young adulthood. Much of the time this process occurs at an unconscious level, but especially in times of transition (attending college, entering into a relationship with a life partner, the birth of children, the death of parents, etc.) people become aware of who they are, and who they are becoming, and how the world perceives them.

Children often look to others as models of whom they might be able to become and what is possible given the resources of their families or communities. This may mean that children consider a wide range of possible "selves" that they might become (e.g., believing parents when they say "you can be anything you want to be as long as you work hard") or, in some cases, it might mean that children begin to understand that there may be limits to what they can achieve, not based on their talents or passions, but based on what might be considered acceptable by the community at large (Oyserman, Gant, & Ager, 1995).

One important aspect of overall identity development is a person's sense of ethnic identity. Elsie Smith (1991) defines ethnic identity as "a learned aspect of an individual's overall personality development" (p. 182). She notes, "through shared historical circumstances, ethnicity serves as a common referent for a sense of peoplehood" (p. 182). Smith notes that people develop their ethnic identity throughout their lives and that it is a process by which individuals decide both how they are *different than* and how they *are similar to* others within their ethnic group and others within the majority culture.

Smith theorizes that ethnic identity development is affected by the status which is assigned to members of the ethnic group by the larger culture (1991). When a person of color is confronted by descriptions of people within his ethnic group that do not match the person's own experience, Smith believes this will lead to identity conflict (e.g., "I am law abiding. Why am I often followed by security when I am in the store?"). Researchers Daphna Oyserman and Kathy Harrison (1999) note that when African American children consider the question of who they are, they most likely will include not only thoughts of who they will become, but who they will be *as an African American*, considering both a rich cultural heritage and negative stereotypes. For those who may identify with more than one racial group, this may be an even more complex process.

Other social researchers have developed frameworks which attempt to explain the process of identity formation for people of color. Most widely known and accepted is Cross's model of *nigrescence* (Cross & Fhagen-Smith, 2001). This model was developed in the 1970s as a framework to understand the process by which an African American might "convert" from an identity that was formed by white European frames of reference (which often reflected a negative valuing of African American culture and identity) to an identity that internalized and was comfortable with being African American. In the ensuing decades Cross continued to strengthen and modify the framework. His ideas now include discussions of those who may not have as much of a conversion from one way of thinking to another, but may form their identity through socialization over a lifetime (Cross & Fhagen-Smith, 2001). A constant in Cross's work, however, is his deep conviction that at some point people of color must wrestle with what it means to live in a racialized society as a member of a less powerful group.

Complicating this discussion is that the traditional understanding about identity formation is that it is an *internal* and an *external* process. A child takes in all the information we have discussed above, frames that information along with his or her own set of understandings and personality traits, and comes to a conclusion about who he or she "is." This process is in keeping with traditional understandings of human development, which were tied to biological development and defined maturity as being self-aware. But recent research points to a more dynamic process where the child's sense of self is formed by both the internal developmental work *and* by how the child believes she is perceived and received by the community. For example, a child may be loved and accepted within his or her family, and may be appropriately protected and supported as she grows, but at some point, she will be challenged by the wider community's norms and values. If the family's loving support is not reinforced by the institutions within the community, this too will become part of the child's self-identity.

Many researchers who have studied adoption note that children who grow up in an adoptive family have special issues in identity formation. Some of these issues may be connected with the reality that as they mature, adopted children deal not only with input from their adopted family and its community and culture (e.g., the question so many adoptees must face early in their lives, "why didn't your *real parents* keep you?"), but also must reconcile who they *might have been* had they been adopted by a different family or remained with their biological family. In past generations, this was an almost impossible question to settle since adoption records were closed and sealed. Emerging standards (such as open adoption) provide an easier path toward answers, but only if the adoptee and the biological parent are both agreeable to such a conversation, and even so, life situations are often so complex that a simple, understandable explanation might not exist.

Identity formation is a long and complicated aspect of development for every child. Upshur and Demick write that for children who are racially different than their parents, identity formation can be even more complex than for adoptees who are adopted in-race (Upshur & Demick, 2006). Transracial adoptees must resolve their feelings about themselves, their parents, and their adoption, as well as the community's response to their "nontraditional" family.

Are transracial adoptees able to manage this well? The results appear mixed. A number of early studies appear to indicate that adoptees are capable of forming strong identities as people of color and that there are few, if any, differences between transracial adoptees and their inracial counterparts (McRoy, Zurcher, Lauderdale, & Anderson, 1982). This appeared to be particularly true in families in which adoption is openly discussed and accepted, when the parents encourage their child to embrace the child's racial heritage, and when the schools and community accept the child (Grotevant, Dunbar, Kohler, & Lash Esau, 2000).

Other studies, however, provide some cautions for transracially adopting families. Several studies have found that children raised transracially report being confused about their racial identity (Feigelman, 2000; Friedlander et al., 2000). One study completed in the United Kingdom, found that mothers of transracial daughters were especially concerned about potential rejection of their children by white grandparents. The mothers feared that the unequal treatment experienced by their children would either be integrated into their children's sense of what they "deserved," which could in turn have a negative impact on the child's own identity, or, conversely, the child might understand that the unequal treatment was wrong, but because of the hurt of being treated unequally might become suspicious of whites in general (Twine, 1999). Some of the parents in our study had similar concerns. One parent in our study noted:

*I would say the extended family dynamics are the most difficult. . . .*
*There are the "real" children and the "fake" children, apparently. My*
*adopted children are not "real" as the core of the family heirlooms are to*

*go to the real children first and then if there's any left, then, fake children may have something to keep. There's a dynamic there that nobody's said anything about. But it makes me keenly aware of our place.*

One parent in our study openly wondered whether her child would be able to form a strong identity as an African American. After discussing how raising a child of color had made her far more sensitive to issues of race, she noted:

*I don't think it was as personal to me as it would be to a black person who has lived with racism much of their life. Certainly I don't claim to have that much empathy. And yet it makes me so happy that the first president my son will know looks so much like him. . . . I don't think if I wasn't an adoptive parent of black children that I would feel that. . . But, it's me, it's this extension of me now. It's a huge privilege to have that identification with another race and culture. So it's changed me in that way, I think.*

Later in the interview, this parent elaborated some more about issues of race and identity. Speaking of her son, she wondered how he would view himself as he became an adult:

*I worry about my child's identity. Will he wonder, "Am I really black if I was raised by white people? What does it mean to be black? Is it just the color of my skin, or is it the culture I was raised in or is it whether I have braids or is it whether my mom has a clue what to do with my hair?" I guess when I think about future things, I guess what I worry the most about, or I think the most about, is them and their own identities.*

Dr. Jean Phinney (1990) has done extensive research regarding how people of color develop and conceptualize ethnic identity. She notes that it is very important for children to develop a well-functioning ethnic identity: both to have a sense of how one is rooted in the history and culture of a group, but also as a way to deal with views of some in the majority culture that may devalue the individual. She writes that ethnic identity is made up of several components. They include:

(1) Ethnic self-identification (if children "correctly" label themselves within a racial group);

(2) A sense of belonging (do children feel connected with the group with whom they have chosen to identify?);

(3) The strength of positive or negative attitudes children might experience towards the chosen ethnic group; and

(4) The degree to which children are involved with cultural and institutional practices associated with the cultural group, (e.g., having friends, attending church, living with others who share the child's ethnicity, participating in political activities that impact the chosen ethnic group). (Phinney, 1990)

Expanding these concepts provides transracially adopting parents important issues to consider as they raise their child.

*Self-Identification* refers to the ethnic label that children use to describe themselves, and for transracially adopted children this can be complicated. For example, what "race" is a child who is biologically Caucasian, Hispanic, and African American, and who is being raised by Caucasian parents? The community may label him African American, but he might label himself as mixed race or perhaps Caucasian. If he spends time with friends who are Hispanic, does he explain or explore his Hispanic heritage? What makes sense to the child? What about his parents? What boxes do they check on the census? And what about the community: does how the child is viewed by neighbors affect the child's sense of self? If at times the community does not see the child as the child sees himself, are the parents aware of this tension, and, if they are aware, what response do they make either inside or outside the family? Do parents provide opportunities for the child to talk about these discrepancies? This process of self-identification is fluid, and parents can assist their adopted child's unique process by being open to the child's developing and shifting sense of belonging within a particular racial group, and accepting that for now, that is his/her identity, even if that's different from prior years, and may shift again.

*A Sense of Belonging*: How strongly connected to the chosen group does the child feel? Young adults often spend time working through how they are "like" their parents and how they are "not like" them; if one of the "me/not me" foci is race, then parents can feel that their children are rejecting *them*.

Children may even reject their biological heritage as a way of fitting into community norms. As Michelle writes in the opening chapter, members of the community may negatively label a child, which can have a powerful effect on the child's sense of belonging. In Michelle's case, she took on the identity of "Egyptian" rather than feel confident in her identity as African American. Talking (often again and again over time) about what this means to a child will be very important to all the members of the family.

***Attitudes toward the Child's Chosen Ethnic Group***: If a child has chosen a group with which he identifies, what does this choice mean to him? Does it provide validation and a sense of security, or is it painful? Sometimes, children may identify with a particular racial group, but not have positive feelings about the group, or may decide that since they are of a particular racial group, they must accept stereotypical understandings of who they are or must become (e.g., since "I am Asian, I must major at math even though I really enjoy writing"). Parents can assist their children by teasing out the *children's* stereotypes as their children begin to make life choices. One family in our study was struggling with these very issues with their middle school aged child who had chosen to identify as black, but whose parents felt that she held stereotypical views of what it meant to be black in her community. Her father noted:

> *Maybe I shouldn't have said this to my child at such a young age, it should be the goal to not live in public housing when you grow up. It's not a good dream to have when you're a kid. What we try to say to our children is: you can do better than this, you can be anything you want to be, you can be a doctor, a lawyer, the president of the United States. They don't see that, and they don't hear it the same way. What they think is you want me to be white. Because they don't see those role models.*

## PARTICIPATION IN ETHNIC INSTITUTIONS AND PRACTICES

Dr. Phinney notes that participation in public events can assist children to feel comfortable with their identity. Some ideas might include learning the language of one's ethnic group, having friendships with those who identify with one's group, participating in religious practices that are ethnically relevant, or participating in political activity or heritage and social events (1990, p. 505).

Children who over the course of their maturation have only slight exposure to groups that mirror their ethnicity may find that such participation has little impact on their identity formation. But others may meet people who can become strong and positive role models. This is another area where parents can have a great impact. For example, if a child is interested in dance, and parents can afford classes, what type of dance classes will the parents invest their money in? If a parent takes their children to the theater, what shows will the children see? If a child is interested in music, what type of lessons will the child have? What type of music is played in the house? What books are parents reading and what books are they reading to their child?

A word of caution: often parents are looking for quick answers or "check lists" of issues that they can address easily and move on to the next important parenting item. This may be because the issues are uncomfortable or simply that parenting is *always* more than a 24/7 job. Parents are already busy simply raising their kids, and these broader issues may seem insurmountably time consuming. In addition, parents often find that if they *do* try to address these issues, their children are not always willing to engage in deep and important dialog. We suggest that rather than this being a "set aside a half day to talk" type of discussion, that parents keep the awareness of these issues in the back of their minds and make small inroads when the opportunity arises.

For example, take advantage of a character or scene in a TV show or movie watched together to discuss stereotypes, behavior, and racial identity. Read books by authors who share the child's ethnicity. Know the history and struggles the ethnic group has experienced and bring up those struggles in casual conversation. For instance, if the child is African American, certainly stop and discuss Martin Luther King, but also include Fannie Lou Hamer, Malcolm X, Sojourner Truth, John Lewis, and some of the leaders in your own home community that are making a difference in a positive way. If the child is Hispanic, know about the struggles of La Rasa, the courageous work of Cesar Chavez, and some of the history of the powerful families that forged ranches in the West before it was a part of the United States. If the child is Asian, discuss the complicated history of Asian exclusion and marginalization as well as how often people of Asian descent are celebrated in the U.S. today. Attending to these racially diverse histories and role models across races, beyond the race of the adopted child, will also potentially build greater respect and acceptance of difference and diversity.

Ethnic identity development is a long (many would say lifelong) process. Do not worry that it isn't "completed." Parents strengthen their children if they are willing to walk alongside them in this developmental journey, and are willing to critically examine how the majority culture has oppressed people of color throughout U.S. and world history.

A special note to parents of mixed-race children: because identity formation does occur over a lifetime, children may form allegiances to several groups over time. For example, one family in which both parents were deeply interested in all aspects of their daughter's ethnicity found that over the course of a decade the child claimed several different ethnicities. Adopted at birth, she had grown up knowing that she was adopted and had been told numerous times of her ethnic heritage (African American, Hispanic, and Caucasian). At age 10, her mother overheard her tell a friend that her ethnic heritage was Middle Eastern, at 12 her father heard her tell other friends of her Native American ancestry. Each time the story was factually corrected in private and birth information retold, and the true heritage celebrated. Not until she reached her 20s was she able to embrace her identity as a mixed race woman; while noting with some irony that the larger community identified her as African American.

A protective factor for children can be family involvement in institutions that recognize issues of race. For example, Angela Brega and Lerita Coleman (1999) completed a study of race and religiosity. They found that children who were more involved in church life were more likely to have black role models and that the idea that the children were accepted and loved by God provided emotional protection from the more stigmatizing messages they received from others. Olivia Williams (2003) also found that especially for African American girls, historically black churches provided a positive institution by which family values were upheld and strengthened. Having wonderful and loving parents is critical, but for children who have been marginalized by race, having both parents and members of institutions available for consultation and support can be a powerful corrective to racism in the larger culture. When families who adopt transracially elect to become part of a church where their children can form relationships with others with whom they identify racially, these trusted friends can also strengthen a child's sense of self.

## SELF-ESTEEM

Researchers Mahzarin Banaji and Deborah Prentice (1994) define self-esteem as "the balance of positive and negative conceptions one has about oneself" (p. 319). A child's level of self-esteem is informed by one's overall identity. As children assess the words and actions of others with whom they come in contact, they will use that information not only to think about who they are becoming, but how the words that are being spoken relate to their understanding of who they are *as individuals.* If what they hear is generally positive, and they are able to manage at least some aspects of their environment (e.g., if they understand and follow the rules, they are rewarded), they may grow in their self-esteem. If children have an appropriate level of self-esteem, it is easier for them to accept themselves and to have the self-confidence to face life's challenges.

In the past two decades parenting books and the educational system have focused attention on this aspect of child development, because research has shown that children with higher self-esteem are more likely to be more confident and more secure in their decision making. Although the concept has been controversial at times, many researchers believe that all children need to feel valued *both* within their families and within society in order to strengthen the child's self-esteem (Halverson, 2012).

As far back as 1989 researchers Jennifer Crocker and Brenda Major noted that members of groups that have been historically stigmatized by the wider culture are most often aware of both the negative stereotypes about their group and the discrimination accompanying such stereotypes. This might lead to: (1) *reflected appraisal* (the child incorporating stereotypical beliefs because they have been shared by people who are perceived as having authority); (2) *self- fulfilling prophesies* (acting in a particular way which reinforces stereotypes); or (3) realization that the rules for the stigmatized group to which the child belongs are different than the rules for other groups in society. All three types of reactions were assumed to have a negative impact on the self-esteem of those in the stigmatized groups.

However, these assumptions were found to not always hold true. Crocker and Major's thoughts are intriguing: they theorize that being a member of a group that is stigmatized may actually provide some "special opportunities for self-protection" (p. 612). The authors provide three potential ways in which a member of a stigmatized group might protect self-esteem: (1) by attributing negative feedback to prejudice against their group; (2) by selectively comparing their outcomes with those of members of their own group; and (3) by selectively devaluing those attributes on which their group typically does poorly and valuing those attributes on which their group excels (p. 612). Having knowledge of the impact that discrimination and historical oppression might play in how one is viewed by the community may provide emotional strength when one is faced with situations that seem painful or oppressive.

Are there particular issues that transracially adopting parents need to be aware of regarding the self-esteem of their children? One important piece of information is that it appears that there is little difference between the self-esteem of children who are adopted transracially and those who are adopted inracially. But the issues that transracially adopting parents face may take a more nuanced approach, and parents should recognize that race may be a factor when children are isolated, bullied, or ostracized.

For example, if a child is not invited to a sleepover with school friends, she could feel isolated and stigmatized. She will naturally seek answers as to why she was not invited. If she determines that she was not invited because she is Hispanic, this might affect her self-esteem negatively, or perhaps she will *devalue the decision of the people planning the party* and label their decision as racism. If that occurs, there is the possibility that her *individual* sense of self-worth will be less affected.

This scenario brings to light another critical reason why transracially adopting parents need to be aware of structural racism and why it is so helpful to have committed friends who are of the same race as your child. Being open to the possibilities that such events can occur will provide parents with sensitivity to the situations when they arise. Talking such painful situations through with your children is far preferable than indicating "what those children do doesn't matter." Of course it matters to your child; and working such issues through can be some of the most painful situations that parents might face. Having committed friends can also assist to balance out this negative situation. Friends can share situations that might have occurred for them as they were growing up. Discussing the hurt as well as strategies they used to deal with the hurt can buffer the pain of not being invited.

## POWER AND COMMUNITY PERCEPTIONS

*Biracial boys tend to be a pretty big threat to Caucasian males in suburban settings. And a little more than biracial girls are. It's kind of "lock your door, here they come."*

When children are born, they are powerless. Children need adults to feed, clothe, and shelter them. They are often seen as extensions of their parents and are accorded status within society according to the status that is held by their parents. During elementary and secondary school, parents protect their children by teaching those skills, directing their choices and in general managing their lives.

Part of growing up is "finding one's place" within the community. This is a gradual process. At first, children share their community status with their parents; as infants, they are often accepted. As children mature, however, they must gradually find their own place in the community. For example, in middle school, parents may be able to intervene in difficult situations, but may not know about every incident that occurs. By the time children are in high school, they have developed their own life and reputation. Even though friends and teachers may be well aware of who their parents are in the community, community members will react to them on the basis of "who they are" and not their parents' status. As adults, most children will have taken on a status within the community that is separate from their parents.

Parents can provide their children with some care and protection, and their hard work also provides the child with what sociologists call *"life chances,"* those things that are unearned by the child but have an impact on who they might become. If a parent has money, holds a position of authority, has a good education, or comes from a family that is respected in the community, a child in that family may have a better set of life chances than a child whose parents are illiterate or live in deep poverty. Although life chances do not completely determine one's life, they do have short and long term impacts: for example, the child of wealth may have better access to good schools, have time and access to extracurricular activities, and opportunities to travel. Those opportunities can further lead to acceptance in college and a choice of career paths.

Parents who adopt transracially have often grown up in families that had such a firm foundation. The parents in our study, not unlike those who adopt nationally, had higher than average incomes and were better educated (75% had completed college) than the general adult population. These parents might expect that their children would have better than average life chances and that they would be accorded society's respect. But many of our parents found that their children were not given such respect; indeed, many reported that their children faced discrimination in schools, at church, and in the community.

Although many parents indicated they had had few if any racially painful encounters, others in our study noted that they and their children seemed to be topics worthy of a public discussion when the children were little. This experience was often interpreted by parents as "simply invasive." One parent noted:

*When you're out in public, people will stop you and they'll start asking just real personal questions. I mean strangers. Amazing how often this happens, because they can see that I'm white and my child's brown.*

At other times, however, transracially adopting parents can bear the brunt of negative scrutiny even when the children are young. One mom who is active in her urban community related this story:

*Well, I've actually had many church experiences. I was asked to do an art program at a mission and showed up early to prepare my art space and had my kids with me and it was the same day the agency was giving out backpacks. Literally when I came to the door to set up, an employee of the agency put her foot in the door and stuck her head out. She didn't want to open the door to me and was guarding the door. She said, "They aren't giving backpacks away for another hour." When I explained to her why I was there, she said, "Well, I'll have to check back with the office." I've had a lot of experiences like that actually. They have already judged you by the time you make it to them. They see you and your group coming.*

One of the realities of such incidents is that parents do not know when they will encounter them. Because these situations might occur at any given time (or not occur at all), it may be hard to "prepare" for them. Thinking together about what to say or not say to those who are reacting to the family and, in developmentally appropriate ways, discussing these issues with children will provide a way to be strong together if these situations occur.

Researchers Joe Feagin and Melvin Sikes (1994) interviewed over 200 middle class African Americans. In their book *Living with Racism, the Black Middle Class Experience*, they noted that even though most of "white" America believes that racism is no longer an issue, for African Americans racism is a *"lived experience"*: something that they felt they must contend with routinely (p. 15).

Most of them had children who were in elementary or middle school. There were a few parents, however, whose children were older; some were now adults and living on their own. These parents brought additional insights into transracial parenting that are often overlooked: the issue of power and prejudice as children mature. What the parents found was that as children matured, and as many of the children's peers were taking on some of their own power and independence, their children of color were often negatively singled out by authority figures such as school officials or coaches.

Transracially adopting parents need to be aware that as their children mature and succeed, that very success may appear threatening to some in the community. In such situations, the child's actions or sometimes the child's very *presence* may cause others to feel threatened. Being aware of this reality and preparing your child for it can be helpful.

Although both young men and young women experienced what parents believed were racist or discriminatory actions, these negative incidences were most often reported by parents when their children were male. One parent noted:

*Dating is the toughest thing, probably the single hardest thing for racially mixed kids. Especially if they are African American and something else. It's a little bit easier if they are Asian. One afternoon, one of our racially mixed kids was in the library. A guy came up to him and just simply said, kind of in his face, he said people like you shouldn't be allowed in here. And used the n-word.*

Another issue is how the community may view a child as he or she becomes an adult. Feagin and Sikes (1994) provide many instances where the men and women that they interviewed were given inferior accommodations, provided bad service at restaurants or ignored, and the person behind them was served even though they were next in line.

A critical area for parents to discuss with their children, especially when raising young men of color, is the overall racial climate in your community. Young men of color are suspended from school, arrested, convicted, and incarcerated disproportionately compared to their white counterparts. Young men of color are also disproportionally stopped for traffic violations. Many social scientists believe that some (and according to some theorists, *much*) of this scrutiny is due to racial profiling and an overall anxiety by the majority white culture regarding young men of color. As noted in the previous chapter, these are examples of what social scientists call "microagressions" and they certainly take a toll on those who experience them. It is not always helpful to assume if "you ignore them they will go away," nor is it always best to confront a stranger who has made an inappropriate remark or gesture.

Parents of color who are raising children know these facts well and have developed strategies to assist their children. These are addressed specifically in chapter eight on communication.

One special note before we close: arming oneself with all the information in the world does not guarantee that you will prevent your child from encountering painful situations. No one, no matter how skilled, can do that! In addition, children may or may not be interested in talking about these situations on a regular basis. As children grow, they are often walking a fine line between "fitting in" and "being unique." A parent's job is to know enough to help if and when they come with questions, and to offer age appropriate opportunities for discussion along the way. We have been surprised about what our children remembered from our own attempts to provide opportunities for ethnic identity formation, growth in self-esteem, and conversations about power. Sometimes we knew we were hitting the mark, other times we were sure that our attempts were being washed away by the emotions of the moment. But each interaction between parent and child, be it a lecture or a hug, the sharing of a book, or attendance at a meeting with a teacher, becomes another piece of fabric in the family quilt and can potentially both be admired when it nears completion and keep your family warm during the dark and painful times that all families face.

This chapter has outlined some important considerations regarding identity, self-esteem, and power that transracially adopting parents should be aware of as they raise their children. But above all, it is important to remember that your love, your openness to your child's dreams, and your willingness to walk with them in both the wonderful and the deeply painful days will be a precious gift to those you love the most.

## SUMMARY

In this chapter, identity, self-esteem, and power were discussed as aspects of parenting transracially adopted children. Universal issues related to these concepts were presented, as well as challenges and opportunities unique to transracially adopted children.

1. Identity Development
   Identity development is the process which happens throughout one's lifetime, but is particularly observable during adolescence and young adulthood.
   The development of an ethnic identity is a portion of this developmental work.

Cross's model of *nigrescence*, explaining the process of identity formation for people of color, is organized around the central tenet that people of color must wrestle with what it means to live in a racialized society as a member of a less powerful group.

Identity formation is even more complex for children who are racially different from their parents, than for other children.

2. Self-Esteem

All children need to feel valued by *both* their families and within society.

As parents of transracially adopted children, it is critical to assess situations, recognizing the possibility of structural racism as an underlying contributor, and to help your child begin to understand this reality.

3. Power

As children grow from infancy, the status they experience within the community shifts from one which is fully shared with their parents, to one which is increasingly based upon both perceptions of who he/she is individually and who their parents are perceived to be. It is not uncommon for children of color to be negatively singled out by authority figures, and their previous place of privilege based upon their parents' identity and position in society has less impact on their daily lives.

## QUESTIONS

1. How might you, as a parent, support your child(ren) in his/her process of identity formation? What resources might you access for and with your child? How might you actively embrace your child's racial heritage?

2. As you parent, what have you noticed about your child's self-esteem? How might you intentionally engage in conversations with your child to support understanding of themselves as individuals?

3. Have you, as parents, begun to prepare mutually agreed upon statements to counter negative or invasive reactions to your family? What steps can you take today to begin to prepare for the inevitable comments, stares, and invasive questions?

4. As you witness microaggressions towards your transracially adopted child, what steps might you take to help them understand

these incidents, and counter the potential negative impact on identity development and self-esteem?

## BIBLIOGRAPHY

Banaji, M. R., & Prentice, D. A. (1994). The self in social context. *Annual Review of Psychology, 45*(1), 297–332.

Brega, A. G., & Coleman, L. M. (1999). Effects of religiosity and racial socialization on subjective stigmatization in African American adolescents. *Journal of Adolescence, 22*(2), 223–242.

Crocker, J., & Major, B. (1989). Social stigma and self-esteem: The self protective properties of stigma. *Psychological Review, 96*(4), 608–630.

Cross, W. E., & Fhagen-Smith, P. (2001). Patterns of African American identity development: A life span perspective. In C. L. Wijeyesinghe & B. W. Jackson III (Eds.), *New perspectives on racial identity development: A theoretical and practical anthology* (243–270). New York: New York University Press.

Feagin, J. R. & Sikes, M. P. (1994). *Living with racism: The black middle-class experience.* Boston: Beacon Press.

Feigelman, W. (2000). Adjustments of transracially and interracially adopted young adults. *Child and Adolescent Social Work Journal, 17*(3), 165–183.

Friedlander, M. L, Larney, L. C., Skau, M., Hotaling, M., Cutting, M. L., & Schwam, M. (2000). Bicultural identification: Experiences of internationally adopted children and their parents. *Journal of Counseling Psychology, 47*(2), 187–198.

Grotevant, H. D., Dunbar, N., Kohler, J. K., & Lash Esau, A. M. (2000). Adoptive identity: How contexts with and beyond the family shape developmental pathways. *Family Relations, 49*(4), 379–387.

Halvorson, H. G. (2012). Forget self-esteem, you need self-compassion to succeed. *Psychology Today.* Retrieved from http://www.psychologytoday.com/em/106630

McRoy, R. G., Zurcher, L. A., Lauderdale, M. L. & Anderson, R. A. (1982). Self-esteem and racial identity in transracial and inracial adoptees. *Social Work, 27*(6), 522–526.

Oyserman, D., Gant, L. M., & Ager, J. W. (1995). A socially contextualized model of African American identity: Possible selves and school persistence. *Journal of Personality and Social Psychology, 69*(6), 1216–1232.

Oyserman, D., & Harrison, K. (1999). African American identity in adolescence. *African American Research Perspectives, 5*(1), n.p.

Phinney, J. S. (1990). Ethnic identity in adolescents and adults: Review of research. *Psychological Bulletin, 108*(3), 499–514.

Smith, E. J. (1991). Ethnic identity development: Toward the development of a theory within the context of majority/minority status. *Journal of Counseling and Development, 70*(1), 181–188.

Twine, F. W. (1999). Transracial mothering and Antiracism: The case of white birth mothers of black children in Britain. *Feminist Studies, 25*(3), 729–746.

Upshur, E., & Demick, J. (2006). Adoption and identity in social context. In K. Wenger (Ed.), *Adoptive families in a diverse society* (pp. 91–110). Piscataway, NJ: Rutgers University Press.

Williams, O. (2003). Effects of faith and church on African American adolescents. *Michigan Family Review, 8*(1), 19–27.

# CHAPTER 7

# Parenting a Transracially Adopted Child with a History of Trauma

## HOPE HASLAM STRAUGHAN

Are there unique circumstances involved in adopting a young child with a history of trauma in general and a transracially adopted child with a history of trauma in particular? If a child is adopted at a relatively young age (between birth and age 3), are there fewer potential issues in the "becoming a family" process, that is, in bonding, trust building, and all of the critical connections necessary to become a healthy family? What are some of the physical, psychological, and relationship-based implications for children who have experienced trauma prior to adoption, and how might an adopting family build skills to support their child? These are some of the key issues which will be explored in this chapter.

## WHO ARE KIDS IN DOMESTIC ADOPTION?

It was necessary within this exploration of transracial adoption to include information on parenting a child who has experienced trauma, as it is a common reality for children who are adopted, even those who are adopted domestically. Many adoptions occur long after infancy, often due to the state or county's determination that the biological parent of the child is not able to raise the child in a safe environment. This removal from the biological caregiver is traumatic for both the child and the parent. When a child has experienced trauma at an early age, there are potentially important implications for that child, and when these issues are overlaid on those explored in other chapters in this book due to the transracial nature of the adoption, there can be an even greater risk of an unsuccessful adoption, or an adoption disruption. The 'otherness' which the child might experience by being the only person of color in a family on top of the tremendous pain and fear the child is carrying from their trauma history can be disruptive, isolating, and more than some parents are able to bear, or manage.

In many situations when children are adopted domestically, the child has been in foster care for some amount of time. Children enter the foster care system due to a variety of circumstances, but almost always because the child has been neglected, abused, or abandoned. The impact of these situations can range from very minimal to quite profound. The circumstances often amount to trauma for young children and, as mentioned in the introductory chapter, it can be very helpful for the family and supporting professionals to both understand and anticipate the behaviors, emotions, and verbal exchanges which might ensue. It is at least as important to begin to understand, in a compassionate way, the reasons for these behaviors, and to resist simply reacting and responding to the inappropriate behavior. It is far better to connect with a child around the *causes* of the actions.

It is not uncommon for an adoptive parent to avoid referring to, recognizing, or talking with the child about any known or suspected abuse or neglect that the child may have experienced. Often parents rationalize this choice because they want to protect their child and focus on the present and future of their new family. They reason that no good parent deliberately sets out to upset the children that they love, and may feel that the child will feel more secure if they leave the traumatic past behind. However, research has shown that children who have experienced trauma, even at a very early age, continue to carry the impacts of this trauma in their bodies and emotions (Van Der Kolk, 2014).

If parents do not ever acknowledge this past, it often sends the message to the child that the past is not okay to talk about, that it is shameful, or even that the trauma is in some way the child's fault. Though in most cases this could not be further from the intentions of the parents, it can add greater pain and difficulty to the child as he tries to make sense of past experiences. Not discussing the past may even impede the attachment process with the new parent.

Adoptive parents are in a unique position with the responsibility and opportunity to help the child acknowledge the events in the past and begin to integrate them into a healthy developing brain, mind, and body. Additionally, parents can serve as advocates for the child as they grow and develop, to ensure that others (extended family members, teachers, baby-sitters, etc.) are appropriately aware of information which could assist the child and avoid triggers, exposing them to situations that would likely be extremely unsafe for the child, given their past trauma. "Sometimes this can allow the people in the child's life to give them the small amount of tolerance, understanding, or nurturing that will smooth the way" (Perry, 2014, p. 5).

Be aware, however, that even when others are made aware of the trauma the child has experienced, it is common for people to become intolerant or insensitive when dealing with the child. In such circumstances, it is okay (and important) that parents take these others aside and help them understand the long-lasting effects of traumatic events and the long process of recovery.

The children's book entitled *Zachary's New Home: A Story for Foster and Adopted Children*, by Geraldine M. Blomquist, is an excellent example of Zachary, the foster-to-adoptee kitten, whose life experiences mirror those of children with a traumatic history (1990). This story holds both the reality of past trauma and loss for the adopted child, and the possibility of being able to bring that reality into the newly forming adopted family and work together to accept, process, and address it. Bruce Perry, senior fellow of the Child Trauma Academy, states that listening to and comforting a child without avoiding or overreacting to the trauma will have long-lasting positive effects on the child's ability to cope with the trauma. It is a way to help a child know that her parent is willing to walk beside her as she sorts out painful issues from her past and places herself within a new family in the present (2014). Before we explore living with and loving a traumatized child in greater depth, it is important to have an understanding of the impact of trauma, abuse, and abandonment on children.

## THE IMPACT OF NEGLECT, ABUSE, AND ABANDONMENT ON CHILDREN

Each year in the United States approximately five million children experience some form of traumatic event. More than two million of these are victims of physical or sexual abuse. Millions more are living in the terrorizing atmosphere of domestic violence. Natural disasters, car accidents, life threatening medical conditions, painful procedures, or exposure to community violence—all can have traumatic impact on the child. By the time a child reaches the age of eighteen, the probability that any child will have been touched directly by interpersonal or community violence is approximately one in three. Traumatic experiences can have a devastating impact on the child, altering their physical, emotional, cognitive, and social development. In turn, the impact on the child has profound implications for their family and community. (Perry, 2014, p. 2)

Such trauma may significantly challenge the child's sense of the world. A flood, tornado, car accident, shooting, or abuse by a caregiver—all challenge the child's beliefs about the stability and safety of their world. Trauma also effects children's perception of everything around them; they often superimpose their trauma on their new relationships and environment. This significantly alters their ability to decipher and understand what is going on around them. At least as troubling is the finding that trauma affects a child's ability to engage in imaginative thinking, exploration, and play, all of which are critical to enhancing the quality of people's lives (Van Der Kolk, 2014).

The issue of safety is critical. Daniel Hughes researches ways to approach parenting children who have experienced trauma (2004). He indicates that an adoptive parent's goal must be to create, reinforce, and maintain a safe physical and psychological space for their child, in all circumstances, even when the child's behavior or attitude pushes all limits, and threatens to upend that safe environment so desperately needed. For example, an adoptive parent can choose to sit on the floor between the child and their sibling or pet, as a protective barrier when the child's behavior has included yelling, screaming, and throwing toys within her reach. The parent should talk softly and quietly, trying to calm the child's racing thoughts and swiftly moving hands, while moving any hard objects out of her reach, and replacing them with stuffed animals, pillows, and socks that can be thrown or even punched, creating a safe outlet for the child's out-of-control behavior. This empathic, loving engagement puts limits on the negative outcomes of the behavior by the adopted child, while keeping other members of the family unit safe, and showing the child by the parent's presence, that she is accepted even when behaving in such a challenging way.

## WHAT PARENTS NEED TO KNOW

In order for adoptive parents of previously traumatized adopted children to parent in healthy ways, it is important for them to both understand the impacts of abuse, neglect, and abandonment on the child, as well as to have strategies to utilize when raising the child. These strategies include creating a safe and stable environment, understanding the power of connection and harmony with the parent, learning about the potential power of body memories and how to support a child experiencing the impacts of them, and reaching out to various resources for support and assistance.

## PARENTS NEED TO CREATE SAFETY AND STABILITY

Children need to be safe and feel safe. Without such actual and perceived safety, researchers have found that the child's neurological, emotional, cognitive, and behavioral functioning is compromised (Hughes, n.d.). When a child feels safe, she is freer to choose to become emotionally attached to her new family. Secure attachment leads to a sense of stability; the child can reliably anticipate that the parent/caregiver will be accessible and demonstrate sensitive interactions (O'Gorman, 2012).

For example, when a young child who has experienced early life abuse and neglect begins to build this securely attached connection with their adoptive parent, she might look urgently to the parent for cues when something surprising or startling occurs, like a very loud unexpected noise or the sudden appearance of a person on the grocery aisle who feels threatening to the child for some reason. The child is looking to the parent to see if they are alarmed, and is seeking to find comfort in the reassuring smile, nod of the head that everything is alright, the soft touch on the back to offer reassurance that the parent is in control, and that there is no need for alarm. This happens naturally for children who develop a strong security base with their caregivers, but has to be developed over time with children who have experienced early life trauma.

## PARENTS NEED TO KNOW HOW TO BUILD HARMONY AND CONNECTION

When young children receive consistent and responsive connections with their mother or primary caregiver, children have stronger health and development outcomes (Snyder, Shapiro, & Treleaven,

2012). The idea of the caregiver's capacity for self-regulation and connection with the child, a way of building harmony with the child, is
called *attunement*. "In a healthy family, a baby forms a secure attachment with the parents as naturally as she breathes, eats, and cries.
This occurs easily because of her parents'/caregiver's bond with the
child. The bond guides the child's parents to notice feelings and needs
immediately and to respond sensitively and fully" (Hughes, 2004,
p. 3). If children are in families in which they do not receive this type
of deeply connected responsiveness, they essentially learn to live with
parents/caregivers who are little more than strangers. "Babies who
live with strangers do not live well or grow well" without some intentional supports and re-working of the attunement bond process
(Hughes, 2004, p. 3). These newly forming healthy attachments can
help children develop trust, a sense of safety, the ability to regulate
their emotions, and even the ability to self-sooth, all of which are
severely compromised when a strong parent-child bond is not created
early in life.

When the child has been removed from her biological parents (and
sometimes has then experienced multiple foster placements before a
final adoption), the adoptive parents must behave in such a way as to
re-work the child's experience of attentive, responsive, and sensitive
attention and trust; what researchers call "attunement." When a child
begins to be attuned to her new family, she can then begin to use the
parent to whom they feel attached as a secure base from which to
explore and seek greater proximity under conditions of stress, danger,
or novelty, as securely attached infants do (Connors, 2011).

This information is important for parents who plan to adopt,
because many adopted children begin their lives in foster families. For
example, in many states, even an infant will be in foster care for at least
60 days until the birth mother and father have legally relinquished
their rights to the child. Even when foster homes are warm and supportive, and the adopting parents are also loving and supportive, the
child has the bonds she has begun to form both to birth mother, then
foster parents, disrupted when the adoption takes place. Two months
seems like a short time to parents, but it is an entire lifetime to a child
who has just begun to experience the world.

In this new era of increased understanding of how the human brain
is designed to work in good relationships, and how such relationships
are central to the cognitive, emotional, social, behavioral, and even
biological development of the person, it is recognized that the parent-
child attachment relationship is central to this healthy outcome

(Hughes, 2009). "At the core of successful parenting practices and optimal child development is the child's secure attachment relationship with his or her parents" (Hughes, 2009, p. 5), based on a context of support, safety, "comfort, and reciprocal enjoyment and sharing" (Hughes, 2009, p. 6).

When children have not received early healthy responses from their parent/caregiver, the child begins to function from a stance of survival and will use whatever behaviors she believes necessary to secure that survival. As noted above, Daniel A. Hughes has developed a comprehensive approach to parenting and/or providing therapeutic support for children who have not experienced healthy attunement in their early lives. His model is based on the premise that the "development of children and youth is dependent upon and highly influenced by the nature of the parent-child relationship. Such a relationship, especially with regard to the child's attachment security and emotional development, requires ongoing, reciprocal, give-and-take experiences between parent and child" (2015, n.p.). The parent is attuned to the child's subjective experiences, makes sense of those experiences, and communicates them back to the child. This is done with playfulness, love, acceptance, curiosity, and empathy.

For example, when a child who has an early life history of abuse and neglect runs across the crowded lobby of a children's museum and hides under the benches, a parent responding in this way might follow the child, sit on the floor very near the child, and instead of lecturing the child on how important it is to stay close to the parent, say something like "It seems like you needed to run to a place of comfort and safety. What does it feel like under that bench?" The very physical presence of the parent near the child, accompanied by this judgment-free, curious observation can lead to a dialogue and physical connection that can calm the child, and allow for a beginning connection in that moment. The repetition of these types of interactions over weeks, months, and years, can significantly assist in the child's development of a sense of harmony or attunement with their adoptive parents.

These interactions are dependent upon the parent initiating an interaction and the child responding to this action, which then determines the parent's subsequent action based on the feedback of the child's observable experience of the first action. In that way, the parent constantly fine-tunes their interactions to best fit the needs of the child.

## PARENTS NEED TO UNDERSTAND THE POWER
## OF BODY MEMORIES

What comes to mind when thinking about important holidays? Do the sounds and smells of a particular season trigger memories? Important memories are not just connected to physical events, but to emotions as well. For example, a person who smells pumpkin pie might remember Thanksgiving dinner at grandma's house even when the pie is baking in July. Such memories are stored in our brains and can last a lifetime. They are called *body memories*. Body memories might be good (like pumpkin pie), or they can be painful: for example a rainy spring morning might trigger the memory of a similar day when the parent attended the funeral of a beloved relative.

When children experience trauma, especially prior to their ability to verbalize, they develop body memories, in which the experiences and emotions are stored in such a way that the person experiences them through sight, sound, smell, and *impression*. Body memories, this ability of the body to hold memories as well as the brain, sometimes causes children with traumatic early life histories to avoid or be triggered by certain smells, sights, places, or sounds without any explainable reason. These memories develop typically when the brain is unable to create and hold the memories, during traumatic experiences in particular. Their traces are experienced in the form of "blind spots" or "empty spaces" in day-to-day living. They manifest themselves in behavior patterns into which a person repeatedly blunders, in actions that the person avoids without being aware of it, or in opportunities offered by life which the person does not dare to take or even to see (Fuchs, 2012).

The child of an author of this book was abandoned during the week of the 4th of July one summer, and for years after the adoption, the weeks leading up to and following that week of the year were very difficult. Each year brought outbursts of difficult and violent behavior. Only after three summers of this experience did the parent make the connection to the very recognizable triggers surrounding this time of year, including summer heat, the sounds and smells of fireworks, and popping sounds of firecrackers. The child was living in a state of anticipation and fear of great threat and loss, given these continuous smells, sights, and sounds. When the parent can identify the causes for the child's behavior (in this case, the imbedded body memory of the trauma of abandonment at this time of year), the parent can work to provide extra support to the child as this event nears, make choices when planning family activities which might minimize the child's exposure to these sights and sounds, and also help to begin to replace the negative body memories with loving, consistent, and safe adoptive family connections and activities.

Hughes's approach is family-based and focused on facilitating the child's ability to establish a secure attachment with their caregivers (Hughes, 2012). Empathy and acceptance of the individual child is central to the child's healing, while also providing him with the comfort and containment needed to explore and resolve past trauma and shame-related experiences, leading to positive, reciprocal relationships with his parents. Within the safety of these new relationships, the child is able to finally face and resolve past traumas. As the child gradually develops a secure attachment with her caregivers, she can also develop a positive and integrated sense of self, which is the goal of such trauma-based work (Hughes, n.d.). When the adoptive parents use the child's name while talking with their child, and use *we* and *us* when discussing shared experiences, these actions have a positive impact on the child's sense of being known and accepted (Oppenheim & Goldsmith, 2007). This sense of being known and accepted is a large part of creating and maintaining a safe physical and emotional environment for the child who has experienced trauma.

In the past few years, there has been an explosion of knowledge about the effects of psychological trauma, abuse, and neglect, revealing that trauma produces actual physiological changes, including a recalibration of the brain's alarm system (fight or flight), "an increase in stress hormone activity, and alterations in the system that filters relevant information from irrelevant" (Van Der Kork, 2014, pp. 2–3). Additionally, the child might simply freeze and be unable to fight or flee, as she is so overcome with the trigger and reminders within her body memories.

## PARENTS NEED TO KNOW HOW TO IDENTIFY RESOURCES FOR THEMSELVES AND THEIR CHILDREN

In some cases, it might be useful, or even necessary, to seek outside therapeutic and supportive services for the child and for the entire family, given early life trauma and its possible impacts on a child. For some children, this level of support might be warranted throughout their growing up years, and can often be a great support to the parents and other family members as behaviors, emotions, and interactions impacted by the trauma play out. The Child Trauma Academy (www.Child Trauma.org), the Annie E. Casey Foundation (www.aecf.org), the Donaldson Adoption Institute (www.adoptioninstitute.org), and the Trauma Center in Brookline, Massachusetts (www.traumacenter.org) all have excellent resources for parents seeking therapeutic assistance.

The brain has an amazingly complex way of altering the synapses and pathways of brain activity due to environmental and behavioral changes, which is certainly possible when children experience abuse, neglect, or abandonment. Much of the work done to support children who have experienced trauma is based upon neuroscience and child development research which provides a greater insight into the impacts on the child's cognitive, emotional, social, behavioral, and biological development (Hughes, 2009). Van Der Kork notes that the brain's own natural ability to be shaped or molded (known as neuroplasticity) can be utilized to help children who have experienced trauma feel fully alive in the present and to move on with their lives after trauma (2014). Three approaches he provides to heal, and possibly reverse the damage of past trauma, include:

(1) *Top down, by talking, (re)-connecting with others, and allowing ourselves to know and understand what is going on with us, while processing the memories of the trauma.*

An example of this type of approach would be when a child who has experienced severe abuse and neglect has developed patterns of excessive control and manipulation as survival responses to her early life experiences. The experienced social worker can work with the child through play and talk therapy to help her understand the causes of her outrageous behaviors. This is not done so that the child is excused for her behaviors, but so she can feel less profound shame for her behaviors and gradually be able to face and shift them.

(2) *By taking medications that shut down extreme alarm reactions, or by utilizing other techniques that change the way the brain organizes information.*

For example, when a child feels unsafe and begins to show signs of hyper-arousal (breathing heavily, reacting to others around her by jerking away from them, yelling, crying, etc.), an attuned parent can work towards interrupting these behaviors, as they actually cause the child to spiral further out of control. The parent might speak with a calm, quiet, loving voice and come behind the child, leaning towards her, rubbing her back gently. As the parent does so, she comes closer to the child, and eventually is standing or sitting immediately behind her, breathing slowly and calmly, and envelops the child in a tight hug which literally serves to contain the chaos that the child is reacting to within her emotions and body. Though the child may fight against the parent at some points in this exchange, the parent lovingly, but with strength, continues to speak quietly and to hold the child tightly as her body begins to respond to the slower breathing of the parent, to the quiet level of the voice, and to the patient and accepting love being offered the child whose emotions were so terribly unregulated resulting in extreme acting out. This process can be quite exhausting for the child, and it is not uncommon for the child to sleep for a little while after such an extended outburst. The parent can curl up and sleep with the child if possible, offering extended care, acceptance, and the gift of presence as the child continues to recover from the experience.

(3) *Bottom up, by allowing the body to have experiences that deeply contradict the helplessness, rage, or collapse that result from trauma* (Van Der Kork, 2014).

Every time adoptive parents look into the eyes of their adopted child lovingly, when they place a gentle, kind-spirited hand on the child's back, shoulder, or head in affection, or give hugs that surround the child with a loving embrace, the child's body is experiencing corrective touch to counter the abuse the child has experienced. It can take years of positive, loving, safe and intimate experiences with family to begin to undo the damaging impacts of abuse and neglect, but each caress, hug, touch, and loving gaze is a significant gift.

Social workers, therapists, psychologists, psychiatrists, pediatricians, and others can assist parents in identifying the best possible approach to supporting their child, addressing the trauma which has been experienced, and helping to create healthy bonds and attachments.

## PARENTS NEED TO KNOW ADDITIONAL WAYS TO HELP THEIR TRAUMATIZED CHILD

Healing, hope, and transformation can be offered to the child who is certain that they cannot be loved, who fears that the abuse and separation experienced in early life is her fault, and who believes she is invisible and irrelevant to everyone else, even their foster or adoptive family. A family must develop a rare combination of internal and external resources if it is to survive the screaming, resistance to attachment, lying, aggressiveness, manipulations, and rage that are often seen in children with attachment disorder. But when families are successful at developing these resiliencies, they will be able to help the child internalize that a safe environment is being provided (Troutman & Thomas, 2005).

What might some of the tools in the family toolbox be that could assist them in this challenging task? They include:

(1) Having an insightful understanding of each parent's *own* attachment history. What traumas or painful situations have shaped each parent's life? What are the implications for the patterns, expectations, and relationship-building or relationship-avoiding strategies which emerge from that history (Hughes, 2009)?

(2) Living in a mindful way: being present in the moment for both joy and pain.

(3) Practicing self-care. One's own emotional, physical, psychological, and cognitive well-being are critical to create the safe and reciprocal environment the child needs. Learn to recognize when one needs a break and then to develop ways to take that break so that children are safe and the parent can relax.

(4) A parent's deep commitment to their marriage, and the relationships with the other children in the family, enhance the child's understanding of safety, stability, and ultimately of trust, that elusive and fragile foundation of healthy relationships.

(5) External community, congregation, and therapeutic resources, including opportunities for respite care, are often absolutely necessary for a family's survival, and ability to become healthy, and ultimately to thrive. Don't be afraid to ask for help!

When a child who has experienced abuse, neglect, multiple placements, or abandonment is placed in a foster or adoptive home, there are varying degrees to which that child will be able to begin to come into harmony and connect with that family. Some children, when provided healthy and loving parenting, are able to learn each day how to engage and connect with their new parent. Others will have greater challenges in connecting with the new parents. These children and families often benefit from intentional and specialized treatment and parenting approaches which are based on the principles of acceptance, curiosity, playfulness, love, and empathy (Hughes, n.d.).

## TECHNIQUES THAT HELP: INSIGHTS FOR PARENTS

The following approaches to parenting and treatment are based on an understanding and integration of attachment and trauma literature:

- Develop a sense of safety by basing all daily interactions on connections made through eye contact, a kind and gentle voice, loving and respectful touch, and interactions which ensure safety.
- On easy days, and on days when it is a challenge to support your child or teenager, be sure to prioritize time for connection through activities that are enjoyed by child and parents.
- With consistency and gentleness, use all opportunities possible to assure the adopted child of your complete acceptance of them and their behaviors and challenges that might be displayed, as a natural outcome of their history of abuse, neglect, or abandonment.
- Set aside previous assumptions about the progress and change that an adopted child might make. Show acceptance and care through patience during a time of little improvement, while celebrating all glimpses of healing and development.
- Even when there is not evidence to support it, remain constant in your belief that your adopted child is doing the very best possible given their experiences in early life.

These parenting tips, though basic in their concepts, can have a dramatic impact on the ability of an adopted child to be able to begin to experience a sense of physical and psychological safety within their new family. This safety will often lead to a sense of connection within the family system. As the child experiences the accepting, curious, empathic, loving, and playful stances of their parents, their challenging behaviors will likely begin to decrease (Hughes, n.d.).

This type of intentional, very responsive connection, reflective of genuine interest shown when interacting with a child or teenager who has not experienced attunement previously, allows for a deeply reciprocal relationship to start to grow, which can begin to shift the internal patterns of being alone and unsafe. Parents/caregivers who discipline themselves to show tremendous compassion in their interactions with the child will begin to open pathways for the child to experience attunement, a sense of matching emotionally with others, and even a sense of resonance and harmony with another human being. This type of interaction, experienced over and over again, is transformative, and allows the child to connect, trust, and learn to build healthy relationships with their family, and beyond.

## SUMMARY

This chapter has provided an overview of the potential impacts of early life trauma experienced by a child who is adopted. Additionally, the implications for the parents of the behaviors, attitudes, and reactions which might be displayed by a child with a history of trauma are explored. The centrality of healthy attachment as a component for the development of trust and safety for a young child is described, as well as strategies for attachment-focused parenting to help introduce a reciprocal, trusting, and persistent relationship with adoptive parents. Resources necessary for parenting children who have experienced trauma, and strategies for interactions were presented.

## QUESTIONS

1. As a parent of a transracially adopted child, do you have information about your child's experiences prior to the adoption, which may include neglect, abuse, or abandonment?
   a. Have you spoken with your child about these experiences? Has your child mentioned anything about these traumatic events?
   b. Have you sought support for your child's processing and healthy integration of these experiences? Where might you find such supports in your community?
2. Daniel Hughes provided the following five parenting/therapeutic principles: accepting, curious, empathic, loving, and playful. Of these, which do you recognize as central to your parenting? Which principles seem counterintuitive and difficult for your style of parenting? Which principles would you like to begin to incorporate in your parenting?

# BIBLIOGRAPHY

Blomquist, G. M. (1990). *Zachary's new home: A story for foster and adopted children.* Washington, D.C.: American Psychological Association.

Connors, M. E. (2011). Attachment theory: A "secure base" for psychotherapy integration. *Journal of Psychotherapy Integration, 21*(3), 348–362.

Fuchs, T. (2012). *Founding psychoanalysis phenomenologically: Phenomenological theory of subjectivity and the psychoanalytic experience.* New York: Springer Science & Business Media.

Hughes, D. A. (n.d.). Creating a PLACE for the special children in our lives. Danielhughes.org. Retrieved from http://danielhughes.org/place.html

Hughes, D. A. (2004). *Building the bonds of attachment: Awakening love in deeply troubled children.* New York: Rowman & Littlefield Publishers, Inc.

Hughes, D. A. (2009). *Attachment-focused parenting: Effective strategies to care for children.* New York: W. W. Norton & Company.

Hughes, D. A. (2012). *Putting attachment theory into practice: Getting through to shutdown children and families.* District of Columbia: Psychotherapy Networker.

O'Gorman, S. (2012). Attachment theory, family system theory, and the child presenting with significant behavioral concerns. *Journal of Systemic Therapies, 31*(3), 1–16.

Oppenheim, D., & Goldsmith, D. F. (Eds.). (2007). *Attachment theory in clinical work with children: Bridging the gap between research and practice.* New York: Guildford Press.

Perry, B. D. (2014). *Helping traumatized children: A brief overview for caregivers.* Houston, TX: The Child Trauma Academy.

Snyder, R., Shapiro, S., & Treleaven, D. (2012). Attachment theory and mindfulness. *Journal of Child and Family Studies, 21*(5), 709–717.

Troutman, M., & Thomas, L. (2005). *The Jonathon letters: One family's use of support as they took in, and fell in love with, a troubled child.* Champaign, IL: The Infant-Parent Institute, Inc.

Van Der Kolk, B. (2014). *The body keeps the score: Brain, mind, and body in the healing process.* New York: Viking.

# CHAPTER 8

# Adoption Communication within the Transracial Adoptive Family

JAYNE E. SCHOOLER AND
BETSY KEEFER SMALLEY

———————————————————————— ⌘

*I know that sometimes a lie is used in kindness. I don't believe that it
ever works kindly. The quick pain of truth can pass away, but the slow,
eating agony of a lie is never lost. It becomes a running sore.*
                                    *John Steinbeck, East of Eden*

Katie, a tall, beautiful, biracial adolescent with a gregarious personality, dark curly hair, and a winsome smile, always celebrated her birthday at the family reunion. This year, now her sixteenth birthday, would be no different. Everyone she treasured as family would be there. However, right after the usual rite of birthday songs and presents, a casual conversation with a cousin forever changed Katie's perception of who she was and how she came to be with her family.

Katie had always known she was adopted. She knew the story inside and out. When she was barely a year old, Katie came to her family as a foster child. She had been told that her mother died of natural causes and that her distraught father could not care for her, left her with a friend, and took off. They didn't even know his name.

That afternoon after the celebration had quieted down, she and her cousin went to the pool. Katie sat dumbfounded as her cousin told her what her mother had just told her—the truth about Katie's birth family. Her mother had not died of natural causes. Her father hadn't just disappeared. What really happened in her past? Both her parents had abused drugs and alcohol. Her mother died of a drug overdose. Her father was still alive, but imprisoned for a long time due to a murder conviction. They knew who he was and where he was. The problem was that everyone in the family knew it, everyone except Katie.

After Katie and her family returned home from the reunion, Katie began to change. She distanced herself from her parents. She challenged their every word. Her parents called it her rebellious stage. They had no idea of what had happened as she kept it to herself.

Katie had always had a lot of friends, and her school performance had been excellent. Both began to deteriorate. She started cutting classes and running with a rebellious crowd. When she was at home she was increasingly moody and sullen. Her angry outbursts frustrated her parents.

Were her parents the problem? Was school the problem? Were her friends the problem? No, the damage was done by keeping a powerful secret. Why wasn't she told the truth? Family secrets . . . haunting words that evoke unsettling memories, disturbing thoughts and uncomfortable feelings. A family secret—something that hides in almost every family cedar chest—information that is banished to a darkened attic, buried under dust and cobwebs, hoping to remain forever under lock and key. What do adoptive family members keep from one another? Why do adoptive families keep secrets? What impact does secrecy have on adoptive family relationships and the person from whom the secret was kept? Why has secrecy shadowed adopted children and their families?

This chapter will explore the broader issue of adoption communication and what children need to know. This chapter will also explore those unique communication needs regarding transracial adoption by offering strategies for parents and extended family.

## THE MANY LAYERS OF ADOPTION COMMUNICATION

When families come together through adoption, a unique set of needs arise around family communication. Families must open adoption communication with their children regarding the circumstances of their adoption and the child's history. Telling a child of his adoption, often a challenge in same race families, is not necessarily an issue for transracially adopting parents. Yet further discussion of the issues that lead to a child's adoption can be. Children who join a family by transracial adoption have their own special needs surrounding their entire adoption story.

# TRUTH OR CONSEQUENCES:
# THE GREAT DEBATE

*Children are afraid of the dark. Adults are afraid of the light.*
Plato, *On Fear*

Adoptive parents have expressed many concerns about talking with their child regarding the child's history, birth parents, and other factors contributing to the placement of a child within an adoptive family. Adoptive or foster parents may be reluctant to share the very difficult circumstances surrounding his separation from his birth family. Sometimes, well-meaning relatives or friends may even advise foster and adoptive parents that what a child doesn't know can't hurt him. The debate can rage on within the minds of adoptive parents, setting up personal struggles. The debate can also impact relationships within the immediate family as family members debate amongst themselves. It is a subject that must be addressed openly, and myths serving to fuel a lack of honesty should be dispelled.

# FEAR OF LOSING THE LOVE AND
# LOYALTY OF THE CHILD

*Myth:* Some parents believe that not telling a child he is adopted is the right thing to do. However, in transracial adoption, that isn't possible, as it is often evident by looking at the children and their parents that they are not fully biologically related. The myth here is that the child will not be tortured by divided loyalties to both birth and adoptive parents if the issue of adoption is never addressed. Some parents might be tempted to distort the truth with stories of birth parents who "died in a car crash" as a way of trying to remove the birth parents from the child's thoughts and loyalties.

*Reality:* One of the paradoxes of parenthood is that when parents try to hold on to their children too tightly, they will only ensure the loss of those children. Those who try to keep their children too close to home when the children are old enough to emancipate, for example, may find that their young adult children decide to move hundreds of miles away. Or stepparents who try to compete for the love and attachment of their children may find that those children turn away from them. Adoptive parents must remember that the child's love of the birth family does not detract from love of the adoptive family. When adopted children are encouraged by secure adoptive parents to acknowledge feelings for their birth families, the children are free to attach to the adoptive family. They are not caught in a competitive, divisive tug-of-war. As Dr. Gorden Neufeld, author of *Hold Onto Your Kids*, says, it doesn't set up competing attachment (2015). By giving them honesty and understanding, adoptive parents give their children permission to love and attach to both the birth family *and* the adoptive family.

Mindy, a nine-year-old child, was adopted at age three. She has only vague memories about her birth mother. Mindy was adopted due to neglect resulting from her birth mother's chronic depression. Mother's Day used to be a troubling day for Mindy as she struggled to honor her adoptive mother without being disloyal to her birth mother. Mindy's adoptive mother recognized her daughter's dilemma and suggested that Mindy write her birth mother a card every Mother's Day, telling her about her accomplishments and feelings, and including drawings and collages about her life. Mindy works very hard on the letters she makes for her birth mother every year, and they are kept in a special album for Mindy to review when she wants to feel close to her birth mother or proud of herself. The understanding and acceptance of the adoptive mother has given Mindy "permission" to love both mothers. Mindy no longer holds herself behind a wall of fear in her relationship with her adoptive mother; she is now free to love her mother because she understands that, to do so, she does not have to stop loving her birth mother.

## FEAR THAT THE CHILD WILL HAVE
## A POOR SELF-IMAGE

*Myth:* Children should not be told that their parents were addicted to drugs or alcohol, incarcerated, abusive, mentally ill, developmentally delayed, and so on. Children will have negative self-esteem if they know their family had serious problems. For this reason, it is acceptable to hide or distort information, or to omit significant facts.

*Reality:* When a child does not have parental support in learning about his history, he is forced to develop an image of himself and his family based solely on misinformation and imagination. What he imagines and is unable to discuss with supportive adults may be far worse than the real situation. Further, it may be the parents' judgments about the circumstances leading to adoption or foster care that could create poor self-esteem. Adoptive and foster parents can learn to present even very difficult information in nonjudgmental ways, giving the child support and love while he is learning about his life circumstances.

Willy, age twelve, was adopted at the age of three following years of neglect by his developmentally delayed mother. His adoptive parents were reluctant to tell him that his parent was cognitively impaired. Willy assumed that his mother neglected him because she did not care about him. Willy's parents shared his history with him when he expressed tremendous rage about his birth mother's lack of concern. Willy understood that his mother had cognitive problems that made it impossible for her to care for her son. With the help of the child welfare agency, the adoptive family was able to obtain information about the extended birth family. Willy finally could feel proud of his ethnic heritage, his birth grandfather's and aunt's artistic talents, and, most important, his birth mother's loving attempts to care for him in spite of her handicap.

## FEAR OF TELLING THE CHILD INFORMATION AT THE WRONG TIME, BEFORE HE OR SHE IS ABLE TO UNDERSTAND THE CIRCUMSTANCES

*Myth*: The child is, and will always be, "too young" to understand prostitution, rape, mental illness, criminal behavior, and so on.

*Reality:* It is true that a small child is not ready to hear the entire story as he is unable to understand the complex social situations that led to his separation from the birth family. Instead, the child is able to understand his life story in layers. What he is told at age three may be a simplified version of reality, with more information supplied when he is better able to understand. The child receives another layer of understanding as he matures, and so on until the child has all the information the parent has.

Amanda, age fifteen, understands today that she was adopted because both of her birth parents were alcoholic and unable to care for her. When Amanda was a preschooler, her adoptive parents explained to her that her birth parents could not take care of her because they were not healthy and were unable to meet the responsibilities of parenthood. As Amanda reached the school-age years, she understood that she was removed from her parents' care by child protective social workers because her parents did not care for her properly. As a middle school child, Amanda learned about the disease of alcoholism and the history of her parents' ongoing struggle with sobriety. As an adolescent, Amanda is learning that her grandparents were also alcoholic. She is being taught about the genetic predisposition to this disease, and her parents are helping her learn strategies to avoid a future of alcohol abuse for herself.

## FEAR THAT THE INFORMATION CANNOT BE SHARED IN A POSITIVE LIGHT; THE ADOPTIVE PARENT DOES NOT KNOW HOW TO TELL

*Myth:* My child will be scarred for life if I don't find the right words to tell him about his past.

*Reality:* Adoptive and foster parents can learn to discuss histories in an age-appropriate, nonjudgmental way. The help of skilled post adoption specialists can also be used when parents feel overwhelmed by very difficult information. While secrets can almost always be lethal, open communication rarely is.

Ben is ten years old now, and his adopted parents believe he has a right to know about his two older birth brothers. They worried about telling him that he was born to an older birth mother, a divorced woman with two older children. They worried that he would feel rejected because the birth mother made an adoptive plan for Ben but kept the older children. The parents decided to take Ben back to the agency that handled the adoption to talk to a social worker about his history. His parents remained with him throughout the interview, during which Ben was able to ask questions about his past and his mother's reasons for seeking an adoptive family for him. Ben initially expressed anger and feelings of rejection. He became interested in his birth brothers, however, and asked his adoptive parents if he might write to or visit them sometime in the future. The parents were supportive of his feelings, and, with the help of the social worker, obtained a picture of the brothers from the birth mother for Ben's room. He displays it proudly on his dresser. As he matures and understands more about the complexities of adult responsibilities, it is likely he will be more empathetic about the reason his birth mother felt overwhelmed by a third child. Because of these fears and myths, parents can be tempted to withhold or change information. The consequences of changing the truth, however, can be devastating to the child and the adoptive family.

## PRINCIPLES OF TELLING THE TRUTH

Whether a child is in a same race adoptive family or a transracial family, there are basic principles that can guide parents in talking with their child about his story.

### INITIATE CONVERSATION ABOUT ADOPTION

Parents often handle discussions about adoption in the same way they handle conversations about sex. They believe they should wait until the child asks questions and answer only the questions asked by the child. This strategy is not helpful in assuring that children understand their histories.

Children often believe that they are being disloyal to the adoptive family when they have feelings and questions about the birth family. As a result, they may avoid conversation about the adoption and the birth family, even when they have burdensome questions or troubling feelings. Adoptive parents must look for opportunities to raise the issue for adoption, and elicit questions from the child. In this way, the adoptive parents assure the child that her feelings are normal and expected, and that they, as parents, do not feel threatened or believe she is disloyal.

There are a number of ways that parents can introduce the topic of adoption within the household and nurture the child's self-esteem at the same time:

1. When a program or movie with an adoption theme is on television or at the theater, watch the program or film with the child. Draw parallels and contrasts between the situation in the program and the child's own adoption. Use this conversation as a springboard to elicit additional questions.
2. Parents can also use key times of the year (often birthdays, Mother's Day, holidays, anniversaries of the placement) to discuss adoption issues. Example:

   *"1 always think about your birth mother on Mother's Day. I'm sure she is thinking about you today too. Would you like to make a card for her and keep it in a special scrapbook?"*

3. Adoptive parents can comment on the child's positive characteristics and wonder aloud from whom the child inherited them. Examples:

*"You have such beautiful long eyelashes. I wonder who in your birth family has eyelashes like yours. Do you ever wonder that?"*

*"You are so good at drawing (music, soccer, math)! Do you wonder if anyone in your birth family is as talented as you are?"*

4. Finally, adoptive parents can comment on the child's accomplishments, including the birth parents in their own feelings of pride. Keep in mind, parents will need to be discerning in terms of talking about birth parents in this context. It might even help to ask the child how it feels when parents bring up birth parents in the conversation. For some children, it might be difficult, for others it might be affirming. The most important thing is that the adoptive parents are interested in and adapt to the child's feelings and questions. Here is an example of a way to assist your child to connect with the past and the present:

*"What a great job! Your birth parents would be as proud of you today as we are!"*

## NEVER LIE TO A CHILD ABOUT THE PAST OR A BIRTH FAMILY MEMBER

Lying about a child's birth parents or history generates serious trust fissures. When the truth is revealed in the future due to a search, a slip by either the adoptive parent or extended family, or an accidental discovery of adoption-related documents, a serious rift in the parent/child relationship occur—a rift which is difficult to repair even with an apology or extensive explanation. What began as "protection" of the relationship with the adopted child can become a "termination" of trust and intimacy in that relationship.

Rachel was removed from her birth family as a toddler due to child neglect. She was placed with her adoptive family when she was four years old. The adoptive family, Orthodox Jews, were very observant of conservative religious traditions. As Rachel grew up, she asked several times if her birth parents were also Jewish. The adoptive family had been told that Rachel's birth family was not Jewish, but they were concerned that Rachel, a strong-willed adolescent, would reject their family's religious and cultural practices if she knew this history. Therefore, they told her that they did not know her birth family's religious/

cultural background and that her family might or might not have been Jewish. Not satisfied at age seventeen with this ambiguity about her birth family's culture, Rachel contacted her placement worker and asked if her birth family had been Jewish. The social worker, not realizing that the adoptive parents had been less than honest with Rachel, shared with her that the birth family had been Protestant. Rachel was much more troubled by her parents' lack of honesty than she was about the information she received.

## ALLOW A CHILD TO EXPRESS ANGER TOWARD A BIRTH FAMILY MEMBER WITHOUT JOINING IN

Many adults remember that as children they became enraged when someone outside the family criticized any family member, even a family member who drove them absolutely crazy! Adoptive and foster parents find themselves in a similar position. They "share" the child with another family without being an "insider" in that family. While the child should be allowed to express both positive and negative feelings about birth family members, foster/adoptive parents cannot echo the negative sentiments.

Many children who are caught up in multiple family systems (stepchildren, foster children, and adopted children) find themselves torn by divided loyalties. If members of any of those family systems berate other involved families, the child's conflict is greatly intensified.

Refusal to join the child's anger can be an easy concept to grasp, but a difficult task to accomplish. After all, many foster and adoptive parents *are* angry at birth family members who harmed their children through substance abuse (during and after the pregnancy), physical and sexual abuse, neglect, abandonment, or emotional maltreatment. When the child expresses anger or outrage, it can be extremely difficult to restrain oneself from sharing that outrage. Maltreatment of a child should never be acceptable, but the adoptive parents cannot allow themselves the indulgence of speaking negatively of the perpetrators.

The following types of comments are acceptable and helpful to the child:

- *"I'm glad that we are able to keep you safe now."*
- *"I can understand why you are so angry."*
- *"That must have been an awfully hard time for you. Is there anything I can do to help you now?"*

Comments like the following are **unacceptable** and potentially harmful to the child:

- *"If your mother had any sense in choosing boyfriends, you never would have been abused."*
- *"I cannot imagine how anyone could abuse a child. They must have been awful people."*
- *"They should lock up your parents and throw away the key. What they did to you was unforgivable."*

## SHARE INFORMATION IN A DEVELOPMENTALLY APPROPRIATE WAY

No one knows better than the parent about a child's ability to cognitively and emotionally make sense of information. Adoptive and foster parents realize that many of their children may have some level of delay due to frequent moves, lack of nurture and enrichment, institutionalization, or trauma. Use language that's easily understood by your child and remember that many children and even teens have limited attention spans, particularly when dealing with painful topics. Several short, simple communications are generally easier for young children to understand than a lengthy "lecture" with multiple messages.

## OMISSIONS ARE OKAY UNTIL AGE TWELVE. BY ADOLESCENCE, ALL INFORMATION SHOULD BE SHARED

The complete history may be too complicated or too "adult" to share with a toddler or even a school-age child. For example, explaining prostitution to a child who does not understand human sexuality is not at all appropriate or advisable. It is sometimes in a child's best interests to learn about his history in increments appropriate to his developmental level.

Parents know their child's developmental level better than anyone. There are no rules about the right age for giving details to a child. This decision depends on the child's developmental level and understanding. Parents must assess each situation individually.

Almost all teenagers, unless developmentally delayed, have the cognitive skills and sophistication to know all of their histories. What do you say to an adopted teenager? The answer is everything. "Adopted people deserve to hear all the facts, all the information that concerns their own lives, their own histories. In other words, an adopted person deserves to know his or her story. So if, for whatever reason, the full story has not yet been told during childhood, it should be told during adolescence" (Severson, 1998, p. 33).

However, most teens appear to believe very few of the things they hear from adults. It is part of the job description of the adolescent to challenge whatever messages come from adults, particularly from their own parents. Therefore, adoptive parents are advised to share information before their child enters the argumentative, stormy stage of adolescence. Paradoxically, children of eleven or twelve will understand and accept information that an older youth might not.

Holly van Gulden writes:

> The instinct of parents who plan to share difficult information is to wait until the child is older, perhaps in their teens. In my experience, this is not the optimum developmental time to share difficult information. Adolescents face two tasks which make processing and externalizing difficult information potentially problematic: individuation and separation. Teens are re-evaluating the question "Who am I?" based in part on their sense of their history to date. Teens are also preparing to leave the family nest . . . this is a critical and complex stage during which to offer new, different, and negative information about the young person's heritage. Though they appear more vulnerable, younger children in middle childhood generally process negative information more easily— not without pain, confusion, and some self-blame, but with less potential for internalizing self-blame/shame for the actions/choices of others. Children ages 8–10 have more time to work and rework material and come to a positive sense of self before they begin to emotionally leave the family nest. (1998, 36–37)

## CONSIDER ASKING INSTEAD OF TELLING

When broaching the subject of adoption or birth family history, a good place to start is by asking questions rather than sharing information. Inquiries about what the child remembers, wonders, worries or fantasizes about will give parents an opportunity to "start where the child is." Some examples of questions that might be conversation-starters are:

- *What do you remember about the time you lived with your birth family (foster family, relative)?*
- *Do you have questions or worries about your birth parents (birth siblings)?*
- *Do you ever wonder about your adoption and how you came to be part of our family?*
- *Now that you are getting older, I bet you have questions about your birth family (how you joined our family). Would you like to talk about that?*

## REPEAT, REPEAT, REPEAT!

Adoption and birth family histories are not "one and done" conversations. The need of repeated conversations increase for the transracially adopted child. As the child matures or develops additional questions, the topic should be revisited. "In order to gain a full understanding of adoption, repeated discussions should take place across time into early adolescence" (Wrobel, Kohler, Grotevant, & McRoy, 2003, p. 59). The child may have misunderstood information previously shared if parents used language or concepts he was not yet able to comprehend. Or the child may have been so focused on one portion of the information, particularly if he has attentional challenges, that he missed other, equally important, parts of the message. Due to his presence in his conspicuous Caucasian family, he may have developed new worries or fears that need to be addressed. Or he may need facts during one conversation and an opportunity to express feelings during another. While parents want to avoid obsessively insisting on adoption communication until the child feels overwhelmed by a barrage of painful discussion, it is important to remember adoption should be addressed throughout the child's maturation. If you can't recall when you had a conversation about adoption with your child, it is probably time to have one!

### Be Realistic, and Don't Paint a Picture That Is Overly Positive or Negative

Some parents, understanding their child's self-esteem is tied to his attitudes and feelings about his origins or his birth family, will describe the birth parents or the situation in such rosy terms, the child may wonder why she was not able to remain a part of the birth family! She may even conclude the birth family was fine, but there was something wrong with her that caused the family to reject or abandon her.

Other parents, particularly those who have adopted children from the foster care system, may have received a great deal of negative information from their social workers. It is only natural that foster and adoptive parents would have negative feelings about people who abused or neglected their child. Foster and adoptive parents should remember the case records have focused on deficits of birth parents, especially in those situations where court cases are being prepared for an involuntary termination of parental rights.

In reality, all parents have both positive and negative qualities, and mature, empathetic adults should help concrete-thinking children recognize both. Furthermore, those children who were adopted at an older age remember times they may have been neglected, but they also remember times when their birth parents tenderly cared for them or played with them. They may be confused when therapists or foster/adoptive parents focus on poor parenting, excluding or ignoring moments of nurture. Duality of positive and negative attributes or memories should be acknowledged, and the child can be helped to understand her birth parents were doing as well as they could, under trying circumstances and with limited resources. However, a child separated from her birth family should also understand all children have a right to a safe, permanent home in which their needs can be more consistently met.

## Don't Try to "Fix" the Pain of Adoption

All parents naturally try to protect their children from pain. However, adoptive parents must recognize that their child must experience some pain in the normal resolution of adoption-related grief. The only way out is through. Do not impose unrealistic expectations that parents can, by saying exactly the right thing, erase all of the pain and sadness caused by separation from the birth family.

When talking with anyone about a serious problem, particularly a loss, platitudes ("You'll have another child." "She was so old—it's better that she's no longer suffering.") are not helpful. Listening ears, soft shoulders, and understanding attitudes are very helpful. Sometimes in parental eagerness to take pain away from children, we instead take away the validity of their feelings. When in pain, children do not necessarily want explanations or reasoned thoughts about what has happened; they only want someone who understands and empathizes, "I know this hurts."

Beth Hall, founding co-director of PACT, an adoption alliance, writes that her daughter experienced a crisis when a storyteller at school talked about the importance of naming. The seven-year-old child told her mother, "I don't think my birth mother really loved me. She didn't give me a name. I wanted her to give me a name." Her mother responded, "I can't imagine how hard it must have been for you to realize that right in the midst of your class." The adoptive mother did her best to listen and support, "not to try to fix, not interpret," the child's grief (Hall, 1998, pp. 20–22). The mother did not give reasons the birth mother might have avoided naming the child ("It might have been more difficult to sign the surrender if she had given you a name."). The adoptive mother also did not try to make her child's pain evaporate by ignoring it or redirecting attention from it ("But you are with our family now, and we did give you a name. So it doesn't matter that your birth mother did not give you a name.").

Often the best remedy for emotional pain is the support that comes from awareness that another person understands and accepts our feelings.


## If the Child Refuses or Resists Communication, Try Again Another Time

Young children generally love to hear their adoption stories. They are naturally self-absorbed, and they love to hear stories about themselves. However, as children mature and understand there are painful elements of grief and loss as well as confusion over divided loyalties involved in their stories, they may become resistant to adoption communication. Parents may wonder if they are overdoing adoption discussions if the child insists, "I don't want to talk about it. Can't you just drop it?" The child's wishes about adoption communication should be respected, and it's certainly difficult, if not impossible, to have a meaningful conversation with an unwilling partner. You can occasionally make comments like, "I'm so proud of the way you handled that tough situation. I bet your birth parents would be proud of you as well," or "Today is a happy anniversary for our family . . . it's the anniversary of the day you became one of us." Occasional references to adoption or the birth family communicate to the child or teen that you are always available when he is ready to discuss the issue.

Some parents report more success in adoption communication if you are in a natural situation where you are not making eye contact with the child. Driving a child in the car is a great time to talk about sensitive issues. Other "no eye contact" moments might occur when playing pool, braiding a child's hair, or going for a walk.

Finally, some adopted youth are convinced they cannot talk with their parents about adoption because "they wouldn't understand" or "they would be hurt if they knew how much I think about my birth family." If an older child or teen continually refuses to communicate about his adoption or history, he might benefit from participation in a support group with other adopted youth near his age. If no post adoption groups exist near your community, seek out foster or adoptive family associations so your teen has an opportunity to talk with other children or youth separated from their birth families.

## Don't Impose Value Judgments on the Information

Information about a child's history may seem very negative, even horrific, to adoptive parents or social workers, but may be interpreted quite differently by the child. As stated earlier, information about a child's history should never be changed, or given to an older child with significant omissions. Facts must be presented, however, without the overlay of values, without judgment.

The child's feelings for or memories of the birth family may alter his perceptions of events. And his need to have positive feelings for his birth family will definitely color his perceptions. If facts are presented in a negative, judgmental fashion, the child interprets this judgment as rejection by the adoptive family of his birth family, his origins, and, ultimately, himself. We do not have the right to judge birth parents; understanding comes from "witnessing" without judgment or censure. Children must develop the maturity to do the same, and this "understanding without judgment" must be modeled for them by the people most important to them: their parents.

This avoidance of judgment can actually be a relief for many adoptive parents. Sometimes, they worry for years about the right time and the right way to present information they perceive to be extremely negative. The child, when presented with the facts, may not see the information as negative at all.

Cameron was conceived as the result of a rape. He was placed as a six-month-old infant with Debbie and John. Cameron had never been told the circumstances surrounding his adoption, and he became obsessed as a preteen with curiosity about his story. His family wanted to protect him from learning, as his own awareness of sexuality was beginning to develop, that his birth father had been a rapist. Not wanting to lie, they simply told Cameron that his birth mother had been unable to raise him. Cameron interpreted this to mean that his birth mother had been a horrible person who had rejected him and found him so repulsive that she could not care for him. When told the actual circumstances surrounding his birth and adoption, Cameron expressed relief to learn that his mother was not a "slut." He understood that his mother had rejected the rape, not him. His imagination had created a far worse scenario than the actual one.

## A Child Should Have Control of Telling His or Her Story outside the Immediate Family

Remember that the history belongs to the child, not to the adoptive parents. If friends or extended family members ask about sensitive information, simply tell them that the information belongs to the child. They can ask him about it when he is old enough to understand their questions. Parents should not decide with whom, when, and how intimate details of the child's life are shared.

Parents may want to assist the child in developing a short, simple version of his story that he feels comfortable sharing with neighbors, school friends and teachers, relatives, and other acquaintances. This "cover story" may be very similar to the information given your child when he was very young. Let the child know that one does not withhold information from acquaintances because it is shameful, but because one should not have to explain one's history in all its detail to anyone and everyone. Explain that some people don't have a lot of experience with adoption and might ask insensitive questions or make ridiculous remarks. At some point, a child will be very grateful to have developed and rehearsed a cover story that will short-circuit these questions.

Liz Clanton and her two children, Peter, age seven, and Katie, age five, both adopted as infants, were sitting in a restaurant enjoying a few quiet moments together. A woman came up to them and commented to Liz about how beautiful her children were. The woman then directed her attention to Peter and asked, "Why did your mother get rid of you?" Thankfully Liz knew that this day would come when her children would need to be prepared to answer uncomfortable questions . . . and prepared they were. Peter, with respect, said to the inquiring woman, "We only talk about that at home." Peter was prepared.

There are two key points to remember when helping a child to develop a cover story:

1. Discuss questions people might ask and the situations the child might encounter. Such things might include introducing the child to a new neighborhood of friends, experiencing the first day at a new school or church, or, as in Peter and Katie's case, what questions curious people might ask at a mall or restaurant.
2. Talk about what information should be shared. It is not an easy task for children to sort out what should be told and what should be kept private. Children can be instructed to provide three basic responses to questions: their name, their origin, and the date they joined the family. It is important for a child to know that he or she is not obligated to tell everyone everything—that there are personal boundaries others must respect.

## REMEMBER THAT THE CHILD PROBABLY KNOWS MORE THAN YOU THINK SHE DOES

Sometimes adoptive parents tell others in the family about "troublesome" details of their child's history, and they believe they will tell the child—but later. No time ever seems like the right time because school is starting, the dog just ran away, or the child just had a fight with his best friend. So parents never get around to telling the child, and someone else does. When information comes to the child from someone other than the parent, the child does not have the support of parents in integrating information into a positive self-identity. And, unfortunately, information is sometimes shared that is not entirely accurate because it has been passed through too many tellings.

Jordan, age sixteen, was placed as an infant with his loving adoptive family. He had two older sisters, both born into the family. Jordan had been born to a woman with significant mental health problems who reported that the father of the baby was African American. Social workers at the placing agency informed the adoptive parents that the baby might be biracial, but certainly did not appear to be a mixed-race child. The mother was described as "unreliable" as a source of information due to her mental instability. The adoptive parents were uncertain about what they should tell Jordan about his racial background. They talked about this dilemma to Jordan's two older sisters, but never spoke to Jordan about the issue. When Jordan and his parents attended a post-adoption support group for parents and adopted youth, the parents were advised to share exactly what the agency had told them: his birth mother, an unreliable source, reported that the birth father was African American. When they did so, Jordan commented, "Oh, I've known that for years. The girls told me all about it." While the parents had agonized over what information to share, their older children had done it for them—not nearly as well as the parents would have handled it. Though the adoptive parents believed that Jordan would eventually ask about his race/ethnicity, he never had. Jordan struggled with identity issues without the support and guidance his parents could have given him.

## STRATEGIES FOR TALKING WITH YOUR CHILD ABOUT RACE AND RACISM

### Listen More; Talk Less

As the authorities in the family, parents often feel that they are appropriately providing guidance and instruction for their children only when they are doing the talking. Yet all effective leaders and teachers have learned the art of listening. Before teaching and guiding, parents must first understand where the child is in his experience, perception, and development. To understand those issues, parents must hear before they speak. Further, parents need to learn more about their child's reality to understand when they can provide help themselves, and when they need to seek help from others. "Parents may tell themselves they feel comfortable raising a child across racial lines, but when faced with issues that threaten their child's well-being, feelings of uncertainty, anger, and perhaps shame can arise. Don't assume your feelings are the same as your child's. Don't overload the situation with your input. If you bring race into every situation to the exclusion of everything else, your child may avoid talking about race with you at all costs. The best advice is: Listen More; Talk Less. You need to understand your child's experience, not direct the action" (Hall, 1998, p. 100).

## Ask Open-Ended Questions

To understand the child's perceptions, parents should not ask questions that can be answered with a monosyllable. Parents should ask, for example, "How did school go today? What happened?" instead of "Did you have a good day?" Use these open dialogues as a barometer to learn more about your child's experiences and stage of identity development.

## Tolerate No Racially or Ethnically Biased Remarks

All parents should teach their children tolerance for diversity. This should include a lack of tolerance for bigotry. When biased remarks are made, these can be challenged in an assertive, but not aggressive, manner. Even if the biased individual's attitudes are not impacted, an important message is sent to all children within the family.

> *As adoptive parents in an interracial or intercultural family, you should refuse to tolerate any kind of racially or ethnically biased remark made in your presence. This includes remarks about your child's race or ethnic group, other races and ethnic groups, or any other characteristic such as gender, religion, age, and physical or other disability. Make it clear that it is not okay to make fun of people who are different, and it is not okay to assume that all people of one group behave the same way. Teach your children how to handle these remarks, by saying, for instance, "I find your remark offensive. Please don't say that type of thing again," or "Surely you don't mean to be critical, you just don't have experience with . . ." or "You couldn't be deliberately saying such an inappropriate comment in front of a child. You must mean something else."* (Child Welfare Information Gateway, 2014)

There may be times individuals within your family or community of friends display harmful biases about your child's cultural group. Relationships with these individuals may become strained, limited, or at the very least, changed.

## Understand You Are a Family of Color

When your family includes children of color, your family becomes a "family of color." As such, you and your family members will be impacted by racism and discrimination. Majority race individuals may not have been consciously aware of *white privilege*, the ability for whites to maintain an elevated status in society that masks racial inequality (Anderson, Taylor, & Logio, 2014, p. 424), and they may be quite surprised and ill-equipped to deal with discrimination, particularly subtle, hidden forms of discrimination prevalent today. Peggy McIntosh writes in her essay, *White Privilege: Unpacking the Invisible Backpack*, "As a white person, I realized I had been taught about racism as something which puts others at a disadvantage, but had been taught not to see one of its corollary aspects, white privilege, which puts me at an advantage. I think whites are carefully taught not to recognize white privilege, as males are taught not to recognize male privilege. So I have begun in an untutored way to ask what it is like to have white privilege. I have come to see white privilege as an invisible package of unearned assets which I can count on cashing in each day, but about which I was 'meant' to remain oblivious. White privilege is like an invisible weightless backpack of special provisions, maps, passports, codebooks, visas, clothes, tools, and blank checks" (1989). When your family becomes a family of color, that oblivion regarding privilege will disappear, and individuals will come face-to-face with discrimination in a way they may find both surprising and disturbing.

## DON'T CREATE PROBLEMS WHERE NONE EXIST

Parents should not constantly search the horizon for racial or cultural problems that do not exist for the child. It is possible to overrespond to the racial and cultural issues faced by adopted and foster children. Parents should not insist on the racial issue throughout every conversation with the child. Part of the delicate balancing act of parenting is allowing for the possibility of conversations, but not always requiring them. Children are not always concealing deep scars or painful emotions. On the other hand, parents should never assume that if children don't bring up a concern, there are no problems.

## DON'T IGNORE ADOPTION ISSUES AND OVER-FOCUS ON RACIAL ISSUES

Identity is one of the issues impacting adopted children and adults. Transracial adoptive parents may be so concerned with addressing racial identity issues, they may overlook the need to address issues of loss, trust, divided loyalties, and so on.

Kevin Hofmann's parents did not discuss issues of either race or adoption within the family. (His story is in chapter five.) Kevin commented, "I always thought about my birth mother, but there was no space to talk about her." When questioned about why he did not ask his parents about his adoption history, he stated, "By not raising the issue with me, I received a silent message that it was not okay to talk about adoption or about race." In the ensuing vacuum, Kevin wanted to know "why she gave me away" and assumed there was something inherently wrong with him. Interestingly, when as a young adult, Kevin decided to initiate a search for his birth family, his adoptive father gave him a large amount of information, "information he had been hanging onto for 20 years."

### CREATE A CODE WORD OR GESTURE FOR DEALING WITH RUDE REMARKS IN PUBLIC

When strangers or casual acquaintances make ridiculously rude remarks in the presence of the child, many families find it helpful to communicate their desire to terminate the encounter through use of a secret code word or gesture. Any member of the family experiencing discomfort can use the word or gesture to let others know that they can no longer abide the stranger's ignorance or rudeness. Children enjoy being a part of the "in group" that knows and uses these codes and can benefit from the camaraderie, implicit support, and fun of using these codes in public. These code words or cover stories can stop the escalation of an unpleasant encounter into a critical incident.

### SUMMARY

Foster and adoptive parents should celebrate the rewards that diversity through transcultural and/or transracial parenting brings into their lives. Few persons of a majority race or culture have the tremendous opportunities for personal growth afforded to those individuals who benefit from this challenge. In summary:

- Be honest and open; it's the unknown that kids can't handle.
- Stay closely integrated in the child's culture. Seek out relationships and connections that will assist your child in maintaining an understanding of and attachment to his or her culture.

- Understand that you are not a white family with some members of other races. You are now a family of color. Remember that as you make choices about neighborhoods, schools, churches, and so on.
- It might be preferable, if adopting/fostering across racial lines, to adopt or foster more than one child of color.
- Don't isolate yourself. You need to socialize and interact with other foster/adoptive families, preferably those with racially mixed families. It is extremely helpful to have other parents to talk with about the issues of raising a child of color to have positive self-esteem and racial identity.

## QUESTIONS

1. What "fear" or worries have you experienced in relation to telling your child the truth about his birth family?
2. Of those fears discussed in this chapter, which is most intense for you?
3. What is the "worst case scenario" if you share information you have been withholding from your child?
4. In what ways does your family differ culturally from your child's birth family?
5. Do you see your family as a family of color? If yes, how has that affected your entire family?
6. Has your child experienced critical incidents? How has he been affected? How have you been affected?
7. What kinds of discrimination might your child experience? Do you feel comfortable assisting your child in coping effectively with discrimination? Where can you find help?
8. Do you need to seek assistance from your child's birth culture to learn ways to enhance your child's self-esteem and positive racial identity? Where might you find that kind of assistance?

## BIBLIOGRAPHY

Andersen, M., Taylor, H., & Logio, K. (2014). *Sociology: The essentials* (8th Ed.). Stamford, CT: Cengage Learning.

Child Welfare Information Gateway. (2014). *Transracial and transcultural adoption*. Retrieved from https://www.childwelfare.gov/pubs/f_trans .cfm

Hall, B. (1998). Grief. *A collection of the best articles on talking with kids about adoption: Best of PACT Press*. San Francisco: PACT Press.

McIntosh, P. (1989). *White privilege: Unpacking the invisible backpack*. Retrieved from        https://www.isr.umich.edu/home/diversity/resources/white -privilege.pdf

Neufeld, Gordon, & Mate, Gabor, MD. (2015). *Hold Onto Your Kids: Why Parents Matter More Than Peers*, New York, NT: Ballantine Books.

Neufeld, G. (2015). The art and science of transplanting children [Training course]. *Neufeld Institute*. Retrieved from www.neufeldinstitute.com

Severson, R. (1998). Talking to your adopted adolescent about adoption. *A collection of the best articles on talking with kids about adoption: Best of PACT Press*. San Francisco: PACT Press.

van Gulden, H. (1998). Talking with children about difficult birth history. *A collection of the best articles on talking with kids about adoption: Best of PACT Press*. San Francisco: PACT Press.

Wrobel, G., Kohler, J. K., Grotevant, H. D., & McRoy, R. D. (2003). The Family Adoption Communication (FAC) model: Identifying pathways of adoption-related communication. *Adoption Quarterly*, 7(2), 53–84.

# CHAPTER 9

# In Her Voice: Angela

ANGELA TUCKER

*In all of us there is a hunger, marrow deep, to know our heritage—to know who we are and where we came from. Without this enriching knowledge, there is a hollow yearning. No matter what our attainments in life, there is still a vacuum, an emptiness, and the most disquieting loneliness.*

*Alex Haley*

Just thirteen years prior to my adoption in 1986, the National Association of Black Social Workers (NABSW) stated that they "stand against the placement of black children in white homes for many reasons" (Chunn & Delany, 1972, p. 4). Their reasons outlined were for our physical, psychological, and cultural well-being and a firm stance "on the conviction that a white home is not a suitable placement for black children and it is totally unnecessary" (p. 4). But what happens when the few black prospective adoptive parents were no longer interested in adoption after learning about my special needs, including the doctor's (incorrect) diagnosis of spastic quadriplegia? What then might the NABSW suggest? By 1994, the NABSW had issued a new statement supporting transracial adoption in the case of a documented failure to find a home with black parents. Essentially, the NABSW deemed it to be more appropriate for me to have remained in foster care for years until all potential homestudies of black families were vetted. I remained in foster care for one year while this search took place without success. Perhaps the members of the NABSW would be pleasantly surprised to learn that my cultural well-being is intact after being adopted by a white couple. Perhaps the psychological difficulties for transracially adopted children lie less within the skin color differences of our parents and more within the trauma of having been separated from our biological parents.

## THE BEGINNING OF MY JOURNEY

I was born in Chattanooga, Tennessee, and adopted at the age of one, at which time I moved to join my new family in Bellingham, Washington. My Caucasian parents adopted seven of my eight siblings, drawing together a family of diverse ethnicities and varying physical and mental special needs. My parents' motivation to adopt stemmed from their involvement in Zero Population Growth (ZPG), a group formed in 1968 that advocates for population stabilization. During the late '60s, and the peak of my parents' involvement, the group feared that population growth in both the developing and developed worlds would ruin the world's ecological systems and threaten the food supply. Of course, this was not the only reason they chose to adopt, but it did factor into their decision on how to build the family that they wanted.

Being adopted under the terms of a closed adoption meant that I was never supposed to meet my birth mother, that her identity was to be confidential, and there would be assurance that my records were forever sealed. At the time of my adoption, my parents were provided four measly pages of non-identifying information about my birth parents. Information included my birth parents' height and weight at the time of my birth, the number of siblings my mother had, her education level, and a statement about her intentions fitting within the realm of altruism and love. The rationale behind closed adoptions was that birth parents deserved a degree of secrecy if they so chose. I am not so sure that my birth mother was ever given that chance to make this choice. I can only surmise that the state hoped that she would forget about me and move on with her life, albeit without any familial support and/or home stability or food. Closed adoptions do not take into account whether or not the bottom rungs of Maslow's Hierarchy of Needs are in place or not. Closed adoptions gained popularity during the World War II "Baby Scoop" era. Closed adoptions are no longer considered to be the best possible option by adoption agencies or attorneys, however some adoptive parents still feel them to be viable options; typically this is to protect their own fears or discomfort.

## MY FEELINGS ON RACE

As I grew I felt ashamed and confused to admit that, as an African American, I "fit in" better within Caucasian communities. In the film *Selma* there was a scene that spoke to me. In that scene, Coretta Scott King is unsure if she has the inner courage to face Malcolm X when he unceremoniously shows up in Selma. While doubting and pondering her courage another character tells her that she absolutely has the inner courage to face Malcolm X. She states that she has it because her ancestors had the courage to bring life into this world; to give it music, love, and country, and still endure when some of those very gifts were ripped away. She reminds Coretta the same blood that flowed through the veins of her ancestors flows through her veins, and therefore courage is in her lineage. I thought about how empowering it might have been for me to hear this sentiment out of the mouth of a black person, a black relative. Perhaps this was what one former president of the NABSW said, "Transracially adopted black children may end up with 'white minds,' which he saw as problematic for the black community because 'our children are our future'" (Jeff, 1988, pp. 1–2).

While I disagree with the NABSW's separatist stance that characterized their 1972 statement, or their modified 1994 statement of a refusal to consider transracial adoption except as a last resort, I concur with their unwritten hopes and feel that white parents wishing to adopt transracially should be willing to be uncomfortable for the sake of their children's healthy adjustment and development. It might mean moving into communities where whites are in the minority so that the children can be surrounded by others who can help guide and mentor them in an organic way. It might mean working to learn to openly recognize the inherent trauma and loss that is as much a part of the adoption story as the joys that may also be present from the creation of a new meaning of family.

In between going to elementary school, attending African American fashion shows, playing with my black Cabbage Patch Dolls, my (Caucasian) sister installing cornrows or box-braid extensions and styling my afro with color-coordinated beads, I found time to write letters to my birth mom. This is a letter I wrote as a teenager:

*Ms. Deborah,*
  *I'm hoping that somehow this letter makes its way into your hands. There are some things I have always wanted to say to you:*
  *I think the world of you.*

*I admire your ability to go through with an undesired pregnancy,
especially without any help, doctors, books, or guidance. I am amazed by
your courage and foresight in knowing that keeping your pregnancy a
secret was the best choice for yourself, and for me. I want to thank you
for thinking ahead enough to find an adoption agency to place me in a
home. I don't know as many people who are as selfless as you who have
the strength to carry a baby to term, walk in to the hospital alone and
in labor, and walk out of the hospital alone and empty-handed.*

*In getting to know you, I do not intend for you to have to retrieve any
painful memories associated with my birth. I hope that you do not feel
any shame for having given me up for adoption. Your strength and
courage to give me up have provided me with more opportunities than
you'll ever know.*

*I'd love to get to know you more.*

*Love,*

*Your birth daughter . . . and by the way, my name is Angela.*

I sent this letter along with annual school photos to the agency that I
was adopted through, under the assumption that the agency was deliv-
ering these letters to my birth mom. Unfortunately, as I came to learn
years later, they sat undelivered in a neglected, dusty file cabinet.

## THE SEARCH FOR MY BIRTH FAMILY

I began expressing interest in finding my birth parents at a young
age. I desired to know the exact reasons my birth parents chose adoption. I wanted the opportunity to have a better understanding of my
ethnic background and had so many existential questions about my
own self that could not be answered by my (adoptive) parents, no matter how caring, intelligent, understanding, or hopeful they were/are. I
wondered where my athleticism came from, and so on. The only information I had in my possession was a four-page, heavily redacted document provided by the adoption agency to my parents at the time of my
birth. That document contained information about the number of
other children Deborah had given birth to, and some statistics about
Deborah (that is date of birth, height, weight, number of siblings she
had, deceased parents). I wondered about my four biological siblings
and whether or not they were adopted too. I wondered about my aunts
and uncles, and how it could be that they never knew about my birth
mom's pregnancy. It became my own nature versus nurture case study.

It's only natural for adoptees to fantasize about moments that no one is able to recount for us. Unsurprisingly, we make up stories that fit the schema and provide some relief for our delicate minds. This is an instinctive reaction for the absence of the truth. Inherent within the business of adoption is the fact that the truth will be difficult to bear. Adoption cannot be synonymous with outright gratefulness and joy. My personal fantasy narratives were that my birth mom may have been addicted to drugs or alcohol when I was born, but that she was probably clean and sober now. Or, likely she was under a great deal of pressure when I was born, but if I had been born just two years later she may've been able to keep me. My parents lovingly indulged in the fantasies with me—up to a point, as they did not want to reinforce any lies. For example, they affirmed the similarities between myself and Magic Johnson when I would loudly declare, "he has a huge smile, and loves basketball, and therefore he must be my birth father!" I watched track star Alyson Felix intently, sure that she was one of my birth sisters, until Google let me know that our birth dates are only one month apart. My parents understood this driving need to make sense of my fragmented reality in this way, while politely helping me to see how those fantasies were unrealistic. I'm glad they didn't allow me to continue to have thoughts that were untrue, but at the same time by dreaming with me they were acknowledging my desire to know where I came from.

I contacted attorneys, paid people who assisted my search, paid monies to the State of Tennessee, and registered with numerous online reunion registries waiting for a match. I grew tired of the injustice I felt in not being able to know my own history, knowing that important pieces of my life were being held and controlled by strangers who did not need this information. I was no longer interested in playing by the preposterous rules. While living in the dorms in college, Bryan (my boyfriend, now my husband) and I would stay up until the wee hours of the morning doing various Internet searches for any of my birth relatives using the very limited information provided. We quickly turned into investigative sleuths, our hearts racing with every phone call, only to hear "I'm so sorry, I cannot be your birth mom because I didn't have a baby girl in 1985" or, "I'm sorry I can't help you, but I wish I could. I have a friend of a friend who is adopted and she doesn't know anything either. I just don't think it's fair."

After focusing almost entirely on my birth mother, we decided to Google my birth father's first name, which someone had accidentally forgotten to white out on a document the adoption agency provided.

His unique name, Oterious, allowed me to do some targeted internet searches, soon finding out that there are only five other people in the entire country with his name. We were quickly able to hone in on one man in his 50s who lived in the city of my birth. A Facebook fan page for a man with the same name provided the first photo I'd ever seen of someone who looked just like me. We weren't able to get in direct contact with him online, but my family and I made the decision to fly across the country to meet this man, who we were quite certain was my birth father.

Many adoptees feel like part of them is missing. I think that this fractured sense of self comes from an adoptee's inability to know their own past, and from folks who aren't understanding of that basic need. After successfully meeting my birth father, we learned that he'd had no idea of my existence. We stared at each other for a long time, unable to believe the situation, but unable to deny the resemblance. Both of us took a DNA test, and enjoyed an awkward, yet incredibly exciting meeting with his/my extended family. Naturally, the conversation steered in the direction of asking him what he knew about my birth mother. He took us to her home, where she denied being my birth mother. I flew home elated and stunned all at the same time.

I couldn't stop wondering about my birth mother. I wondered if she even cared about me, or if she chose adoption because she was forced to . . . questions spiraled around my head for a full year before my phone rang. It was my birth mother. We arranged another flight out to Tennessee where she agreed to meet with me and to introduce me to my other siblings. During this trip we visited the agency to which my parents had been sending the timeless gifts of pictures and letters, and were able to give all of them to her at once.

My birth mother said that she had always wondered what happened to me, where I grew up, whether I was ever able to walk, and what my family was like. She was not concerned that I had grown up with white parents, but was simply glad to know that I'd been loved and that I wanted to know her after all of these years.

## CONCLUSION

I imagine that it's hard for some people to imagine why I would spend so much time on this project. No one seemed to understand what I felt when people exclaimed, "You look just like your mom!" or

"You totally have your dad's eyes, but your mom's nose," and so on. I couldn't have felt more isolated and alone during those conversations with my peers. I have always wondered what it felt like to have your family history always at your disposal, or to know your genes and be able to trace your ancestry.

School assignments often added to the pressure, as I was repeatedly required to complete a family tree in class; I would routinely use my (adoptive) family, but problems arose when I was asked to trace physical characteristics. So much of my energy has been freed up since finding my birth mother. I no longer look at every older, black female and debate whether or not to go up to them and ask if they birthed a child in the '80s for whom they then chose adoption. I no longer need to weigh the appropriateness of my desire versus their rights. The exhausting subconscious habit of looking at every single female who vaguely fit the description ceased to exist. It's difficult to truly understand the magnitude of the task of an adoptee choosing to search for birthparents. Adoptees inevitably feel pressure to balance expectations on both family sides—assuring birth parents you aren't angry/upset with them (even though you may be), but also assuring adoptive parents you're not searching in an effort to replace them.

A great majority of parents receive praise when they first announce that they are expecting, in the hospital delivery room, or perhaps the praise extends in to and through the terrible twos, but the awe and reverence typically stop there. But not so for my parents. They still continue to receive praise today. They are given names such as "Saint Mother Teresa," "Savior" or "God-sends." Thankfully my parents, realizing the inappropriateness of the statements deflate the compliment with a response of "No, we are just parents." They say this in the same tenor as they might say "It's dinner time!"—calm and matter-of-fact without any punctuated emphasis on any certain word. Their deflection and refusal to accept this praise helps my personhood not to feel so unnatural. The inherent meaning behind those compliments has to be that there is something about me that is especially difficult to parent, something that is worthy of only a *saintly* parent. My parents embraced the attitude that without knowing my full trauma history, I'd continue to feel as though I didn't belong. It is for this reason that they supported me in my search to better know my identity and find my birthparents.

For more information about Angela and her story, visit www.theadoptedlife.com and www.closuredocumentary.com.

# BIBLIOGRAPHY

Adoption History Project, The. *Transracial adoptions*. Retrieved from http://www.uoregon.edu/~adoption/topics/transracialadoption.htm

Child Welfare Information Gateway. *Transracial and transcultural adoption*. Retrieved from http://www.childwelfare.gov/pubs/f_trans.cfm

Chunn, J., & Delany, L. (1972). *National Association of Black Social Workers position statement on transracial adoption*. Atlanta, GA: NABSW.

DuVernay, A. (Director). (2014). *Selma* [Motion picture]. United States: Studiocanal.

Evan B. Donaldson Adoption Institute. *Finding families for African American Children: The role of race and law in adoption from foster care*. Retrieved from http://www.adoptioninstitute.org/publications/MEPApaper200 80527.pdf

Jeff, M. F. X. (1988). President's message. *National Association of Black Social Workers Newsletter, 1988*(Spring), 1–2.

# CHAPTER 10

# Conversations with Practitioners: What Adoption Professionals Want Parents to Consider

## JANE HOYT-OLIVER

*I just wish there was a way to convey to parents that they cannot enter an adoption [without considering hard questions] because they want a family so badly that they just want to create it in a hurry.*
                                                                S.F., *adoption caseworker*

Adoption is wonderful and difficult, exciting and painful. There are times of absolute joy and other times of great uncertainty. That is, of course, similar to *all* parenting experiences, but as mentioned in earlier chapters, parents who adopt take on additional challenges as well. For one thing, the biological processes are different: the emotional connections that one makes to a new child do not begin with the biological connections between mother and child in the womb and rarely with the experience of watching with growing wonder your partner's pregnancy. Instead, parents begin to emotionally attach after birth and, most often, after some months or years have passed in the child's life. This is a reality that all adoptive parents must understand and embrace.

Adoption is also different because it often involves the presence of social workers, lawyers, and even others (e.g., birth parents) in the process. It is a public process that differs significantly from biological pregnancy. Potential adopting parents are interviewed to determine whether they could be good parents to a child. Parents are asked about their own life story and evaluated to ascertain their ability to support a child emotionally and financially. They are asked many questions about their physical and psychological well-being and how they plan to parent. In so many ways, people who would like to adopt a child are scrutinized by professionals who determine not only which children might thrive in the couple's family, but even if the couple is a candidate for parenting an adopted child at all.

Children who are placed for adoption come to the adoption process with their own life stories even when they are adopted as infants. They have begun their lives in the womb of another who may or may not have wanted to be pregnant. They may have been cared for as they developed in their biological mother's womb, or may have been sorely neglected. Once born, they may have lived for a while with their biological parent or been placed in foster care. They may have been nurtured, or painfully abused. All children have their own life experiences and those life experiences will lead someday to a set of questions which the child may or may not choose to ask. Each child is a unique life and each, *from birth*, begins to live their own unique life history.

Although most of this book has incorporated the stories of parents who have adopted transracially, the authors felt that any such book for adopting parents should also include some information we have gained from talking to adoption professionals. It is critically important that adoption workers think carefully about each child and try to match that child's needs as closely as possible with the desires and gifts of the potential adoptive parents. These women and men are legally charged to act as advocates for children and to work within the legal system to assist parents hoping to adopt find a forever family. Their work is done within the confines of both state and federal laws, which can regulate a wide variety of adoption related issues (Carter-Black, 2002).

Most, but not all, laws mandate that workers keep the "best interest of the child" at the forefront; however, there are often competing interests at work: adopting parents, biological parents, foster families, and, of course, the children themselves often have a great deal at stake in the adoption process. Even within the laws governing adoption, tensions exist. For example, one important piece of legislation, the Multi-Ethnic Placement Act of 1994 prohibits agencies receiving Federal monies from denying any person the opportunity to become an adoptive parent solely on the basis of the race, color, or national origin of the adoptive or foster parent or the child involved (Bradley & Hawkins-Leon, 2002, p. 233). Although the law was intended to broaden the options for children in the foster care system to find permanent homes, in practice workers report that its regulations can stifle the worker's ability to ask questions about parents' understandings of race and culture. Do those who work with adoptive families every day have concerns that they might want to share with parents?

Adoption professionals were interviewed to get a sense of what they think transracially adopting parents might want to consider and what, in their experience, some of the pitfalls and joys of adopting transracially might be. Many of these workers had decades of experience. We share this information with parents in hopes that the issues that are brought forth here will provide guidance for them in the role of parenting a child by transracial adoption.

All the professionals we interviewed were passionately committed to finding loving homes for the children placed in their care. The workers had between three and ten years of professional adoption experience. Some had assisted with only a few transracial adoptions during their careers, but others had assisted with more than 80. Several of the adoption professionals were employed by public agencies; others were employed in private faith-based and secular nonprofit agencies. Two of the agencies focused specifically on foster care and adoption; in the other two agencies, foster care and/or adoption services were only one aspect of the overall agency mandate.

The professionals who specialize in this work believe strongly in the adoption process. As one worker put it, "A child needs a home. Period." Another worker noted, "I feel permanency is above and beyond the most important thing for a child." These professionals worked towards finding matches that are in the best interest of the child and are informed by the laws which guide their work.

Even if one is simply contemplating adoption, we encourage each prospective parent to read through this chapter carefully. It is in this chapter that the reader will see what professionals want parents to know before they adopt, and some of the issues that they would hope that adopting parents would consider as their children grow. As an adoption professional stated:

*I feel like sometimes [parents] don't know what they don't know. They don't know the questions to ask. They don't know what this might be like and I think unfortunately there are a lot of obstacles to being able to talk to them about that.*

One thing that all of the professionals stressed in our interviews was the importance of the initial placement of the children with the parents. They wanted to make certain that "good" matches between potential parents and adoptees were completed. However, this was not the *only* thing that mattered. The professionals understood that it was also part of their job to consider how parents might address the needs of children as they grow. Trying to think into the future life of parents and children is always difficult; when one adds race and adoption into the mix, adoption workers know that special sensitivities are needed; often love is *not* enough.

## IN THE BEGINNING

The process of being matched to a child for a potentially adopting parent can be complicated. As noted in a previous chapter, many parents consider adoption usually as a second choice after they have been unable to expand their family biologically. They deeply desire to welcome a child into their home; indeed, some parents talk about the time between deciding that adoption is an option and the time they bring a child home as a "desperate" time. It is just during this vulnerable period that potential adopting parents must answer many difficult and invasive questions posed by adoption professionals. There is sometimes a great temptation to minimize issues that could be painful for parents and children later on.

As part of the screening process, potential adopting parents answer questions about who they are, who they want to be, and aspects of a child's history that they are willing to incorporate into their own family. In light of their overwhelming desire to bring a child into the family, some of the most invasive topics may be glossed over either in discussion between each other, between the adoptive parents and all members of the extended family, and *even within the individual hearts* of each adoptive parent.

One of the authors remembers reviewing the "checklist" with their spouse and trying to make a decision about accepting a child who had sight impairments, who was deaf, or who had developmental delays. These questions caused them to ask not only questions about who a potential child might be, but who *they thought they might be*. What issues might they be capable of addressing? What issues might they resent? And, to be honest, if they were going to be resentful about a child's needs, *what does that say about who they were as people?* They wondered about the professionals who would determine if they were accepted as potential adoptive parents: *how would they be viewed by the professionals.* Their emotions pulled them in so many directions; they were concerned if they were too selective, perhaps they would be seen by the social workers as too selfish to care for a child at all. Conversely, if they wrote that they were open to a child who had, for example, multiple developmental issues, would they be truly able to nurture and raise the fragile life that might be entrusted to them? Many evenings of honest and sometimes painful discussions accompanied that list back to the agency. It was a humbling experience.

The adoption professionals we interviewed understood that transparency is critical in every step of the process. They recognized that parents who indicate they are interested in transracial adoption should think about the challenges that their new family might encounter. One professional noted:

*I don't think parents culturally think about down the road because the adoptive child is a newborn baby. The parents think, "We'll get there someday" but I don't think they always think about the culture and how they are going to incorporate [the child's] culture [into the family life].*

Another professional added:

*People in the larger community automatically see skin color . . . even though that shouldn't be the way things are, it does happen. I just think it's very important for parents to examine their own thoughts and feelings and how they grew up. They need to look at their neighborhood, look at the schools in their area, and that type of thing. They should think about their friends and their social interactions such as the church [they attend]. Parents should question whether the race of their child is truly going to be an issue.*

To assure the best possible connection between both the potential adoptees and the adults who long to care for them, radical honesty on the part of the couple hoping to adopt is needed. Radical honesty occurs when parents tell themselves the truth about their community: not the truth they want to believe (e.g., "Our church loves everyone, so of course our child will be accepted and treated well," or "of course our school system will welcome our child"). Radical honesty does not come easily, because it requires parents to transcend their own desires, perceptions, and expectations and focus instead on the individualized needs of a child. It means rebalancing older family norms, history, and traditions to include rituals that would be grounding for a child. It is realizing *everything needs to change* if a new life enters an established family unit. One professional put it this way:

*Adopting parents need to think not only "how am I going to feel about this" or, "how is my family going to feel about this," but really how is my child going to feel about this and how is my child going to be perceived. I really do believe that when a transracially adopted child is not in their parent's presence, they are perceived very differently than they would be if they were the family's same-race child. I think a family really needs to be intentional about it.*

Initial questions that every parent considering adoption should ask include: What can I give to a child? Am I willing to give even when there is little support from extended family or community institutions? Do I have the ability and desire to care long term for a child who may have complex needs? As noted in previous chapters, not all adults can cope with the day to day realities of living with a child who has already experienced significant trauma. What behaviors might challenge or hurt at a very basic level? When these behaviors occur, how will parents manage the behaviors in a way that will be acceptable while providing their child with guidance and stability? If these behaviors occur, do the parents know if some members of the extended family might fault the child's race rather than the trauma as the underlying cause? And, most importantly, might *the parents themselves* be capable of potentially destructive race-based thinking?

The time to be radically honest begins at the very beginning of the adoption process. Parents need to ask themselves if they can be proud of their child and his or her racial heritage. One worker painfully recalled an interview with a couple who had recently adopted a biracial child:

*I had a family that refused to tell the child that she was biracial. They were going to pass her off as a Caucasian child and I remember clear as day sitting in their kitchen saying, "Listen, this is not a good idea," and they were just very against it. I said, "your child is going to know" and the parents replied, "she'll never know." The parents basically refused to take the child's life story from me and were going to hide it. When will the child find out about this? Eventually she'll find out, she'll find out. And there goes all of your trust right out the door.*

The decision by the adoptive parents not to share the truth with their child described above may have been rooted in a desire to protect the child from racism, or to protect the parents from having to deal with race within their family. Perhaps this choice was a way in which the parents believed that they could pretend that their child was not adopted. But as the worker stated, the decision not to share such an important reality with their child will critically undermine the child's trust when the child discovers the truth.

## THOUGHTS ABOUT EXTENDED FAMILIES

As earlier chapters in this book have established, parents who adopt transracially have additional issues to consider even beyond those experienced by all parents. Adults who are considering creating a trans-racial family need also to thoroughly discuss how they will address issues of race within their family and with extended family members. As the parents whom we interviewed so clearly demonstrated, having extended family support is not *mandatory* but it is clearly helpful. When times are painful, when children are acting out, and when adults are at the end of their emotional rope, turning to relatives who are both wise and supportive brings strength to parents. If extended family members cannot or will not support parents at such times, or if they cite the race of the child as contributing to the overall concerns expressed by the parent, those parents may experience an increased sense of isolation.

Parents whose extended families were either overtly or covertly hostile to their transracial family did find support from other sources, such as the couple who formed a group of supportive friends who met regularly to talk about parenting and adoption. Groups such as these can become extended families of choice over time. But knowing that this will be a concern before one adopts provides a context for an adopting couple to consider coping strategies if the extended family is unwilling to provide support. What is critical is that adults consider-ing transracial adoption think honestly about their families (including any other children who are still at home or young adults on their own) and how the potential adopting adults plan to address transracial adop-tion with those they consider family.

When potential parents are longing for children, there can be a tendency to believe that love will overcome the greatest obstacles, or that "somehow things will all work out." People who adopt have often had good relationships with their families of origin, and have learned to work around the negative aspects often experienced between broth-ers, sisters, or parents. Parents considering adoption need to resist the temptation to engage in "magical thinking"; that the family members who have expressed racist views will "change" once they get to know the children, or that somehow the parents' love for the child will be a sufficient shield against the potential racism of extended family members. One professional related the following:

*Extended families don't always buy into it. For example, one parent I worked with adopted three African American children. The mom's parents were not pleased with the idea. Her parents lived out of state so she didn't see them a lot, so that helped the situation. They knew that she fostered children, but after the adoption, she still had not told them yet. Mom's parents just thought the children were still there as foster children.*

The parent in this situation loved her children and wanted to protect them. But the mom's decision not to "rock the boat" with her extended family for the sake of "family harmony" could eventually backfire. There could easily come a time as the children grow that they will become aware of this deception, and may, in fact, be asked to perpetuate it. Perceptive children will be aware that their parents find the confrontation too difficult and could conclude that the potential anger of the extended family is more powerful than the bond between the child and the adopting parent. Such deception is clearly a short term solution that could lead to long term insecurity for the adopted children: they may wonder in what *other* situations might mom or dad choose peace with the relatives over honesty about the children's adoption?

A better solution might be for adopting parents to be up front with their extended family, addressing the concerns of relatives, expressing their own, and setting boundaries early about what might or might not be tolerated. Dialoging together about the strengths and limits of one's extended family and what choices the adopting couple will make on behalf of their new transracial family can provide for a rich and honest discussion, which can set the stage for positive parenting.

Adoption professionals often observe that families have not fully thought these issues through. Because they care deeply about finding permanent and loving homes for each child on their caseload, adopting parents can expect that caseworkers will ask challenging questions. One professional recounted:

*I wish parents knew from the beginning the importance of embracing the child's culture, not ignoring it. I wish they knew about the child's needs whether it be skin, hair, knowing all of this beforehand. Where do their friends, family, and support system stand with it? There was a scenario I had where a family had wanted to be matched to a biracial child. It stated on their checklist they weren't accepting of African Americans. Biracial, but not African American and the child was Caucasian and African American. I didn't want to accept the family because the home study stated that their family and friends would not be accepting of them adopting an African American child. So I asked them "Half of this child is African American and you're sitting here telling me you're not willing to consider an African American child. What makes you want to consider a biracial child?" And they said, "Well, celebrities are adopting more and more African children, so I think my friends and family will just accept it." I want them to know ahead of time that you can't make all these assumptions. You can't just say, "Oh well, they'll accept it because it's our child." They need to know beforehand how their support system is going to respond.*

In addition to thinking honestly about extended family members, adoption professionals wish parents would think about how their family will be perceived in public. One professional quipped:

*Parents need to be prepared to field questions in unintended intrusiveness. Now, that's going to happen to the family that is a bunch of dark-haired, European types that adopt a child with red, curly hair, too. Anybody who's perceived as not belonging is going to be questioned by somebody at the grocery presuming that it is their business. I think in some ways, there's a general adoption piece to it and in some ways that really is relevant to families that adopt transracially.*

## AS CHILDREN GROW

To parents who have been blessed with a child who will expand the forever family, Congratulations! As most parents quickly discover however, the screening process, the initial adoption, the post adoption visits, and the finalization hearing are only the beginning. Parents often are excited and relieved about the gradual withdrawal of agency oversight, and at finalization they feel they have "passed the test" and can be a family "like any other." At one level, parents understand that every family faces trials and tests as they raise their child, but after such in-depth scrutiny, many believe they are prepared.

Because they have been evaluated, interviewed, and visited by adoption professionals, for the most part at finalization they are ready to move on from formal relationships with the adoption agency. Adopting parents often believe things are going well enough, and do not remain in contact with the adoption agency even when their adoption workers reiterate, "Please do not hesitate to call if issues arise." Parents may feel that to call the agency after finalization is to admit that parenting is difficult, or that they are somehow inadequate parents. Some may believe that the issues they are facing are "just part of parenting," and that if they are "good" parents, they will be able to figure a way through their difficulties without formal intervention. Others may even feel that if they were to call, it would be tantamount to "admitting" that the agency had made a mistake and that they were not adequate to parent the child entrusted to their care. If they are in positions of authority within their community, they may be concerned that their family business will become community business. Reflecting on this reality, one professional mused:

*I think there's also an element of fear prior to the finalization of, "oh, my gosh, I can't let the worker know that we're having an issue or there are issues and I don't want to ask too many questions, because I don't want to upset the apple cart and I can't risk losing this child."*

All the professionals interviewed for this book expressed a willingness to assist parents, to provide resources and make suggestions. Several noted that when children are adopted at a young age, issues of race are often part of family conversations, but less an issue in the surrounding community. Adopting parents may not have too many issues when their child is young, but as the child matures, community prejudices may become evident.

Some of the agencies provided support groups for families, and the agencies that did not had the names of support groups and other resources at hand in case families would call. It *is* ok to ask for help. It *is* ok to ask questions. Learning to love a child often means that we have to move beyond our own comfort zones for the sake of another more vulnerable human being. Adoption workers are committed to helping children find a permanent home, a loving "forever family," and are more than willing to assist new parents with their questions. If a parent is unsure of what is needed, remember to ask those who might have some answers.

Parents who adopt transracially can face additional issues. If they have not been trained about the differing hygiene needs of their children, for example, they may not utilize appropriate care for the child's skin and hair. If the parents are living in a predominantly white community, parents might not be given good information or even be able to purchase appropriate products for this care. Learning where these products can be purchased, even if they must be purchased online and delivered, sends a powerful message to a child that he or she is accepted and cherished for who the child is. If parents cannot find these products in their community, one option would be to ask store managers to stock them, but managers might refuse, believing there are too few people in the community who would purchase the products.

One of the adoption workers interviewed spoke of one family living in a rural and predominantly white community. She noted:

> *Mom can tell you where every hair care product she has needed for her child can be found within like a 10-mile radius of her. She'll make special trips once a month to come into the closest urban area, but sometimes I've gotten some insight from her for other families. I don't know where to buy the products myself. I mean, I would say, go to a Wal-Mart or Target, but in her community they don't even have it at the Wal-Mart and Target.*

For some transracially adopting parents, even a monthly trip to a community that might have the hygiene supplies needed by their children may be difficult. However, in the 21st century, parents have many options, such as ordering appropriate products online. The critical first step is knowing that such products are needed and knowing how to use them correctly, unless your child is old enough to take care of these issues by him or herself.

During the training that comes before adoption, professionals do provide a good deal of information to prospective parents but noted that in the high-stakes nature of the adoption process, prospective adopting parents often appear to not really take in the information provided. Prospective parents are so focused on the outcome (being considered eligible to adopt) that they perceive the information about culture, grooming, and potentially difficult racial issues as secondary to the adoption itself. One worker noted:

> *I think during the training piece a lot of information goes in one ear and out the other. Potential adoptive parents are enamored with the process, and they want to get down to the end, and then they want to get babies.*

*I think it's important to continue to have the conversation with adoptive parent about what they are facing today and what they are going to face tomorrow. Are you OK with having that conversation with Mr. and Mrs. So-and-So about the hair of your child? . . . Can I hook you up with a salon that I know?*

In addition to the "selective listening" that may occur during training, the day to day demands of parenting can also obstruct a parent's ability to address these broader issues. Parenting children is *always* challenging, and as noted in earlier chapters, children who have been adopted *at any age* have special issues that will complicate bonding. Parents can become overwhelmed with the day-to-day realities of raising a child. This, coupled with the insecurities discussed earlier, may lead parents to think they will be viewed as inadequate if they don't handle issues solely within the family. In many cases, the parents resist contacting the agency for help.

This reality is not lost on those professionals who work in adoption. When asked in her "heart of hearts" what percentage of transracially adopting parents need more information about how to cope with the impact of structural racism and privilege on their families, one worker replied:

*Probably the majority of them. . . . I would say, "We can give you mentors if you need help with hygiene or hair care or understanding with certain cultures or understanding a certain race." They're going to need a melting pot of friends and colleagues and support groups so that their kids can have somebody they can look up to, some of whom look like them. To answer your question how many people do you think reach out, I don't think a lot, because we have an adoption support group and most of the people that we have in our groups are not people that adopted through us.*

Another concern for adoption professionals is how to assist all members of the family to lean into that delicate balanced dance of personalities that allows families to thrive. One worker with four years of adoption experience commented:

*The biggest challenge for adopted kids is just struggling to fit in— finding their place in that family and in that neighborhood and in that extended family while wondering if the parents still viewed them as their adoptive child instead of saying their child.*

Adopting parents often focus on what strengths they bring, and how those strengths might benefit a needy child. Parents dream of sheltering their newest member, and bringing nurturing and strength to a vulnerable life. They may be less inclined to consider how *they* may need to change: how they may have to alter their food, clothing, or music choices to accommodate the needs of their child. The truth is when parents adopt transracially, the family itself becomes a transracial family. Some professionals feel that adopting parents don't spend enough time talking about the impact that might have; if they are willing to take on the realities of living in a racialized society. One worker noted:

> *I just think it's very important for people to consider the child's thoughts and feelings, not just the parents, and not just the extended world but the child too. Sometimes they might be hiding their feelings and not bringing them out. Make sure their feelings are being considered—whether it's in therapy or whether it's just within the family.*

Another professional who assists agencies to find appropriate adoption matches explained:

> *I often hear workers say, "How are you going to expose adoptees to their culture?" Culture is something learned. You can keep the subscription to* O *and* Ebony *magazine, but will they see faces like theirs? Will they go, to a school where they see faces like their own? Will they have places where they can glean some wisdom that they won't get in their homes? I have heard parents say, "I wasn't raised between the knees of my mother braiding my hair while my father talked about what to do when a police officer stops you." I think it's something that they really ought to be required to contemplate. Before you make this decision, I think that, professionally, I wish there was more room to talk to families about why they decided to do a transracial adoption.*

As the professionals quoted above attest, thoughtful and honest reflection doesn't "just happen," but is a choice deliberately made by parents to insure that the new life that has been brought into the family will come to trust, in time, that they are welcomed by other family members and that the new family member is not required to be the only one that must adjust to new circumstances. Transracially adopting parents need to consider what they read, what they watch on TV, and where they shop. They may want to set aside money and time to attend plays and art exhibits that help them and, when appropriate, their children to learn about the experiences of people who are identified as being of the same race as their child. Such experiences provide for increased cultural sensitivity and a truly multicultural perspective to the truly multicultural family that is being created. Such experiences lead to opportunities to strengthen the bonds between family members. For example, before the advent of widespread online shopping, one parent found that the high-end department store in her community did not carry makeup that blended with her teen daughter's skin tone. She then arranged a "special" biannual trip to a mall 75 miles away so that her teen-aged daughter could get the makeup she needed to participate with her friends in the "makeover" parties that were popular at that stage of the child's life. This trip became a special time of connection for both. The parent noted that, although it was unspoken at the time, she knew she was reinforcing to her daughter that the daughter was fully accepted for who she was, and as parents she and her husband would do everything in their power to demonstrate that *all* of who their daughter was would be honored and celebrated within the family.

These extra challenges take place as children are maturing. The children (both developmentally and as a consequence of adoption) are also deciding how to negotiate a place within the family. The truth is that there may be periods of time when a child wants nothing to do with the "adoption story," electing to focus on how she or he is *connected* in the family. It is also true that for some children, the reality of adoption is painful and they simply feel "different" than how they imagine their friends that are biologically related to their parents might feel.

Children may go through periods when this connection is a primary need and then have other periods when they desire to celebrate and explore their cultural roots. So, the best a parent can do is to be *open* to talking, and *prepared* to do so. Here are more suggestions:

- Learn more than the basics about the history and culture of the child's heritage.
- Develop a natural, ongoing conversation about what you have learned or are exploring.
- Listen for windows when the child wants to talk about issues of race.
- Talk to friends or coworkers about what parents might need to know: and assume as a new parent you have much to learn.

- Be open to exploring some of the deeper realities of structural racism with your child.

For example, Jasmine was in advanced placement classes in her large, urban public high school. The school offered an African American History course, but not at the AP level. If she took African American History, even if she got an "A" in the course, both her class rank and her overall GPA would be lowered because AP courses "counted" more in both categories. That lower rank, in turn, could affect college admissions and scholarships, which were important for the entire family's well-being. This was something that her parents discussed with Jasmine asking what her preference was regarding which course to take and the long term and short term consequences of each choice. The parents affirmed to their child that they were willing to stand by her whatever choice was made. In addition, they spent some time discussing how such standards are set (in this case, state rather than local school board mandates) and how assumptions about "what's important" and "what's worthy of advanced study" by the decision makers within the majority culture can be translated into a student's lack of knowledge about other important subjects.

When children are young, their world will orbit around their parents' world. As children mature, and their own world expands, they begin to make their own world on some levels, but parents still have remarkable influence. Parental decisions as to where to live, where to worship, where to shop, and even how political events are interpreted continue to be a great influence on a child's understanding of himself within his community. One professional, noting the impact that these decisions have on a child, stated:

*Will your children see faces like theirs? Don't tell me, "I have friends that are black." Do you ever go to dinner with them? Are they ever in your home? Do you go to church with them? Do you live, go to a school, and play on baseball teams with them? Will [your child] be the one black kid in the choir? You know because that stuff is hard.*

There is a good deal of emotional balancing that goes on as children mature. Often there is a mash-up of human development, emotional development, family dynamics, and personality, as well as race, culture, and adoption issues that come into play in any one interaction with a teen or preteen. Parenting at this stage is often daunting, perhaps even overwhelming for both parents and for teens. Keeping lines of communication open whereby children are free to speak about hurts and concerns and where parents can be honest as well can smooth out some of the rougher times. As one professional noted:

*When I have parents that adopted older children there's . . . always that sorting out of, is this adoption related, is this because I'm white and he's black, is this because he is a teenager? So, he had a thousand texts on our phone bill. OK, that doesn't have anything to do with the fact that parents transracially adopted, but so you're sort of always sorting it out. Yeah, I hate the music he listens to, it's all rap. OK, but would you have liked heavy metal any better, you know? So, I'm not sure that's a transracial issue or a teenage issue.*

In any family, these can be confusing times for parents. Having good and wise friends can be essential supports for parents who must walk with their teens through adolescence. Parents who have adopted transracially can further find support from friends who share the same race as their children. One professional who is also a transracially adopting parent of teens shared this story:

*You would think I would know you can't prepare parents. I have more than once been around a person who expressed frustration and/or a biracial person who was not adopted but kind of doesn't know where they fit. I've come away feeling sometimes . . . I'm damned if I do and damned if I don't. I don't know how to make this better. I'm never going to be good enough for society to parent this child. One of my friends and colleagues who happens to be a black woman said, "God, I love you for even saying that out loud and don't worry about it. You know, you are enough." I wish there was a voice for the parents that says they're enough. You are enough. Which is why I come back to the idea that you can raise your kids to be morally sound and give them a foundation of awareness and respect and audacity that underpins so that they can manage better a [racist] situation that comes.*

## RELATIONSHIPS WHEN CHILDREN ENTER LATE ADOLESCENCE: PARENTING FOR THE FUTURE

The early adult years can be times when parents and children set down the stories that will define how the family will see itself in the future. Although it is difficult in the rough and tumble day to day grind of parenting, it may be important to set aside time to anticipate together what developmental issues may need to be addressed. One worker noted:

> *I think parents need to look at what's happening in our culture and what's happening in our society and kind of plan ahead, you know, and not put blinders on and not be surprised when your next door neighbor says something racist. The child has to be given permission to come home and talk about it and with the understanding that the family knows that, yes, this is happening and it's not something they're making up.*

Again, this is a time in which radical honesty needs to be predominant. Parents may be relinquishing power, but this is typically a slow process, some of which includes formal agreement (e.g., "use the car as long as you complete your chores," or an agreement about curfew times on nights and weekends) and some of which may be informal. But in many situations transracially adopting parents need to consider the effects of their actions on their children and consider the overall consequences for the family. This can include discussions about dating and marriage. One professional noted, "with some families that could get to be an issue as to what race are you going to date, what race you are going to marry." One family discussed this issue with their daughter, noting that the parents would welcome any person that she dated. As an aside, they noted that their primary concern was that she be loved and respected. Further, they noted that whoever she chose might have *parents* who might voice concerns about their transracial family, but that to the fullest extent that her parents could control the situation, they would see that as an issue between the two sets of parents not between the couple.

There are many other issues that arise for families in which creative solutions may need to be found to otherwise routine family changes. For example, in one transracially adopting family, the father, who worked for an established non-profit agency with several regional locations, was required to move from a diverse urban community to a rural community 20 miles away, that was more than 90 percent white. Their child was a junior in high school and a student leader. Meeting his new staff before the move, the father noted that although the rural high school was well regarded, their child would remain in the urban district for senior year. In advance of the meeting, the family had weighed the effect of this decision (seen as a "lack of commitment to the community" by some) with the effect on their child and chose in favor of the child's needs.

When children are young, parents are in charge of most major decisions. As children grow, ideally, parents gradually relinquish some decision making (e.g., *what do you plan to wear to school?*) to their children while maintaining control over other decisions (e.g., *what time must you be at home after a date?*). Parenting is often a dynamic dance with elements of protection, nurture, fear, pride, and humility. Although parenting an infant is seen as the primary time for protection, parents who raise teens can admit to watching a teen attempt to painfully navigate the rocky waters of maturity. This brings forth fierce protective instincts. By the time a child is in his or her teens, parents will have their own stories of race and culture. Some may be wonderful and some may be painful. But they are the family's shared stories and they will set the stage for how race and culture will be addressed within the family as adults.

Adoption professionals are aware that parents are parents, and they are simply creating the connection that brings families together. But they are ready to assist, to guide, and to provide resources that can help parents and kids at any stage of a child's development. So, at any time in the life of your child, take the time to be aware when you might need some advice, and then be willing to connect with those who might be able to help. As one adoption professional noted:

> *These kids come with different experiences and when they're older they may have different issues that you're not used to and so the adoptive family needs to be open to helping these children. It's just not going to be feed them, love them, and life's going to be wonderful. They need to be prepared for that.*

## BIBLIOGRAPHY

Bradley, C., & Hawkins-Leon, C. (2002). The transracial adoption debate: Counseling and legal implications. *Journal of Counseling and Development, 80* (4) 433–440.

Carter-Black, J. (2002). Transracial adoption and foster care placement: Worker perception and attitude. *Child Welfare, 81*(2), 337–370.

# Appendix: Resources for Further Information

## WEBSITES

### GENERAL INFORMATION

www.child.tcu.edu: Trust-Based Relational Intervention from Dr. Karyn Purvis.

www.empoweredtoconnect.org

www.neufeldinstitute.com: "Hold onto Your Kids" and much more.

www.nctsn.org: National Child Trauma Stress Network.

www.theraplay.org: Theraplay© Institute.

http://blog.leeandlow.com/: This book seller lists books for adopting families by the age of the child. Includes books for single parents who adopt and books for families that adopt children from other countries as well as more general books for children about adoption.

https://adoption.com/forums: Discussions by both adoptive parents and parents considering adoption.

https://www.childwelfare.gov/topics/adoption/adopt-parenting/foster/transracial/: An informational site with links to many topics of interest to adopting parents.

http://theadoptedlife.com/: Angela Tucker, author of Chapter 9, blogs about her experiences.

### ISSUES OF RACE AND JUSTICE

http://www.christenacleveland.com/: Cleveland, writing from a Christian perspective, eloquently discusses race and justice in the United States.

# RECOMMENDED READING

*Adoption in a Color Blind Society* by Pamela Anne Quiroz
*Adoption Nation: How the Adoption Revolution Is Transforming America* by
     Adam Pertman
*Be My Baby: Parents and Children Talk about Adoption* by Gail Kinn
*Beyond Consequences, Logic, and Control* by Heather Forbes
*The Boy that Was Raised as a Dog* by Dr. Bruce Perry
*The Connected Child* by Dr. Karyn Purvis
*Growing Up Black in White* by Kevin D. Hofmann (author of Chapter 5)
*Hold Onto Your Kids* by Dr. Gordon Neufeld
*Inside Transracial Adoption* by Gail Steinberg and Beth Hall
*The Interracial Adoption Option: Creating a Family across Race* by Marlene G.
     Fine and Fern L. Johnson
*The Out of Sync Child* and *The Out of Sync Child Has Fun* by Carol Kranowitz
*Parenting from the Inside Out* by Dr. Daniel Siegal and Mary Hartzell
*Racism in the United States: Implications for the Helping Professions* by Joshua
     Miller and Ann Marie Garran
*Theraplay©: Helping Parents and Children Build Better Relationships through
     Attachment-Based Play* by Phyllis B. Booth and Amy M Jernburg
*Transracial Adoption Today: Views of Parents and Social Workers* by Lucille
     Grow
*Weaving a Family: Untangling Race and Adoption* by Barbara Ann Rothman
*The Whole Brain Child* by Dr. Daniel Siegal
*Wounded Children, Healing Homes* by Jayne Schooler, Betsy Smalley, and Tim
     Callahan

# ADDITIONAL READING RESOURCES FOR ADOPTIVE FAMILIES AND PROFESSIONALS

*After Adoption: A Manual for Professionals Working with Adoptive Families* by
     Jean Pierre Bourguignon and Kenneth Watson
*Ambiguous Loss: Learning to Live with Unresolved Grief* by Pauline Boss
*Journeys After Adoption: Understanding Lifelong Issues* by Betsie Norris and
     Jayne E. Schooler
*Nurturing Adoptions: Creating Resilience after Neglect and Trauma* by Deborah
     Gray
*Talking to Your Child about Adoption* by Patricia Donner
*Telling the Truth to Your Adopted or Foster Child: Making Sense of the Past* by
     Betsy Keefer Smalley and Jayne E Schooler
*Twenty Things Adopted Kids Wish Their Adoptive Parents Knew* by Sherrie
     Eldridge

*The Whole Life Adoption Book* by Jayne E. Schooler and Thomas Attword

## BOOKS FOR CHILDREN AND TEENS

*Answer Me, Answer Me* by Irene Bennett Brown. Bryn Kenney's search for
    her parents begins after the death of her Gram, when she is unexpect-
    edly provided with a fortune and a clue to her roots.
*How I Was Adopted* by Joanna Cole
*Is That Your Sister? A True Story of Adoption* by Catherine and Sherry Bunin.
    A six-year-old tells what it's like to be adopted in a multiracial family.
*Mr. Rogers: Let's Talk about Adoption* by Fred Rogers. Confronts questions
    children have about adoption with sensitivity and insight.
*A Place in My Heart* by Mary Grossnickle,
*Teenagers Talk about Adoption* by Marion Cook
*Who Is David?* by Evelyn Nerlove
*You Be Me, I'll Be You* by Pili Mandlebaum

# About the Authors and Contributors

JANE HOYT-OLIVER, MSW, PhD, is chair of the social work program and teaches social work and social welfare policy at Malone University in Canton, Ohio. Jane grew up in a family with both biological and adopted children. She and her husband transracially adopted their daughter as an infant. They have spent their careers primarily in rural and suburban communities.

HOPE HASLAM STRAUGHAN, MSW, PhD, is associate dean for Social Work, Leadership, and Policy and teaches social work at Wheelock College in Boston, Massachusetts. She and her husband transracially adopted their two sons when they were preschoolers, and as a family the two sons remain very close to their other biological brothers and their adoptive families. Her areas of research and practice include spirituality within social work practice, human rights and justice-based practice, and foster care and adoption. She grew up in the West and has lived on both coasts before landing near Boston.

JAYNE E. SCHOOLER, MBS, has worked for many years as an adoption worker and trainer in Ohio. She is the author/coauthor of numerous books related to adoption, including *The Whole Life Adoption Book*, *Telling the Truth to Your Adopted or Foster Children: Making Sense of the Past*, and *Wounded Children, Healing Homes: How Traumatized Children Impact Adoptive and Foster Parents*. She and her husband adopted their son when he was in his early teens. She has spent most of her adult years based in western Ohio, but has traveled extensively nationally and internationally as a trainer in child welfare. In the past decade she has been involved in the development of international adoption and orphanage caregiver training in Mexico, Ukraine, Kyrgyzstan, Haiti, India, and other nations. She is a full-time staff member of Back2Back ministries, headquartered in Mason, Ohio.

KEVIN HOFMANN is an adult biracial transracial adoptee who works as a trainer for the Ohio Child Welfare Training Program. He trains foster parents, adoptive parents, and child welfare professionals on the joys and challenges of transracial adoption. Kevin is also a CASA (Court Appointed Special Advocate) volunteer working with and advocating for children in the foster care system. In addition to these responsibilities, Kevin works as an in-school diversity consultant working with school districts in the areas of diversity and inclusion. It is his desire and passion to help pave a path that is easier to walk for transracial adoptees and families, as well as giving all children the tools to walk through life respecting all and being respected.

BETSY KEEFER SMALLEY, coauthor of *Telling the Truth to Your Adopted or Foster Child: Making Sense of the Past* and *Wounded Children, Healing Homes: How Traumatized Children Impact Adoptive and Foster Parents*, has 43 years of experience in child welfare, adoption placement, post-adoption services, and training. *Telling the Truth* received the Pro Humanitate Award from the North American Resource Center for Child Welfare in 2000 as the book making the most significant contribution to child welfare in that year. Betsy works presently as foster care and adoption training manager for the Institute for Human Services in Columbus, Ohio.

MICHELLE OLIVER works as in-house counsel and director of human resources and risk management for a manufacturing company based in the Midwest. She was transracially adopted as an infant by Caucasian parents. She is a graduate of Kenyon College and Case Western Reserve University's School of Law, where she concentrated in International Law. While a law student, she worked for the UN International Criminal Tribunal for Rwanda in Tanzania, as well as the International Criminal Court in The Hague. She practiced litigation at two large Cleveland-based law firms before joining her present company. Most summers since she was in her mid-teens, Michelle has participated in mission outreaches overseas, traveling extensively in Ghana, Mozambique, South Africa, Brazil, India, Indonesia, and

Singapore with Frontline Ministries International. This nonprofit and mission work has been extremely meaningful to Michelle, in particular, working with both orphans and victims of human trafficking. In her spare time, Michelle enjoys working out, hiking, exploring the local food scene, mentoring youth, and participating in community outreaches with her local church.

ANGELA TUCKER is a transracial adoptee and the subject of the documentary *Closure*. Angela has been a keynote speaker for highly acclaimed events, including the annual conference for the American Academy of Adoption Attorneys, the State Department of Colorado's Annual Convening for Judicial and Family Court Teams, and the American Adoption Congress. Angela is a contributing author for several books and publications, as well as an editor and columnist for *The Lost Daughters*, an all-female adoptee contributor website, and has been featured as a commentator on CNN's *Anderson Cooper 360*, *HuffPo Live*, *The New York Times*, and the *Washington Post*. Angela works full time as a disability advisor at her undergraduate alma mater, Seattle Pacific University.

# Index

abandonment, and children, 95–96

abuse: by having control of story telling, 124–125; children and, 95–96; communication refusal by children, 122–123; consider asking instead of telling, 119–120; early life, 97; fear of losing the love and loyalty of the child, 111–112; fear of poor-self image of children, 112–113; fear of sharing information, 114; fear of telling the child information at wrong time, 113–114; information shared a caregiver, 96; sexual, 95, 117; substance, 117

adolescence, 118–119; children entering late, 156–158

adoption: choices within, 16–17; communication within the transracially adoptive family, xvii; educating extended family on, 33–34; and grooming, xvi; initiating conversation about, 115–116; issues in, xii; pain of, 121–122; race and, xiii–xiv; reasons for, xi–xii

adoption communication: being realistic in, 120–121; children by adolescents, 118–119; children expressing anger, 117–118; initiating conversation about adoption, 115–116; layers of, 110; lying about family members, 116–117; omissions allowed until age twelve, 118–119; pain of adoption, 121–122; repeated conversations, 120–126; sharing information, 118; strategies for talking to children about race and racism, 126–129; within the transracial adoptive family, 109–130; truth or consequences, 111; value judgments imposition, 123–124

adoption constellation, 33

adoption laws, 49

adoption professionals, 141–158; and adoptive parents suitability, 19; views of, xviii

adoption triad, 33

adoption-related grief, 121

adoptive children. *See* transracially adoptive children

adoptive parents, 94, 96, 111–113; additional ways to help their traumatized child, 103–105; in adoption study, 17–19; avoidance of judgment by, 123; building harmony and connection, 97–99; challenges of, 43–44; creating safety and stability, 97–99; identifying resources for themselves and their children, 101–103; insights for, 105–106; preparation of, 19; suitability of, 19;